James Roderick Moir, born on 24th January 1959, Leeds, West Riding of Yorkshire, England, UK, better known by his stage name **Vic Reeves**, is a comedian, artist, musician, actor and TV presenter, best known for his double act with Bob Mortimer as 'Vic and Bob,' along with his surreal sense of humour. Reeves and Mortimer were listed in The Observer as one of the 50 funniest acts in British comedy during 2003. In a poll to find the Comedians' Comedian in 2005, Vic and Bob were voted as the 8th-greatest comedy act ever by fellow comedians and comedy insiders.

James took an apprenticeship in mechanical engineering at a factory in Newton Aycliffe after leaving school, before later moving to London. He also formed the Fashionable Five, a group of 5 friends, including Jack Dent, who ran the original Fan Club, who'd follow bands including the Enid and Free onto stage, performing pranks, like Moir pretending to have a brass hand, also following a Terry Scott lookalike around Darlington town centre in single-file formation. They later formed their own group, James having an early breakthrough with the help of comedian Malcolm Hardee.

He began a part-time course at a local art college during 1983, developing his liking for painting, persuading a local art gallery to stage an exhibition of his work. Although still best known as a comedian, Moir has a growing a reputation as an artist, his drawings and paintings having been used on his TV shows, forming a large part of his book, Sun Boiled Onions (1999).

As well as working and performing in bands in London, including being an original member of the Industrial/Experimental group 'Test Dept', going onstage with them at their debut gig then leaving soon afterwards, James joined the alternative comedy circuit under many different guises. These included a loudmouthed American called Jim Bell, a beat poet named Mister Mystery then 'The North-East's Top Light Entertainer'— Vic Reeves.

His stage show Vic Reeves Big Night Out began as a regular Thursday night gig at Goldsmith's Tavern, New Cross, later the New Cross House. There, he met Bob Mortimer, a solicitor who attended the show, enjoying it so much that he soon began to take part. Moir's TV début was in December 1986 on Channel 4's 'The Tube', in a comedy game show segment called Square Celebrities, being suspended by a wire to ask the 'celebrities' questions.

His next appearance was on the short-lived chat/comedy show 'One Hour with Jonathan Ross', in a game show segment known as Knock Down Ginger. James's growing TV profile led to Big Night Out being given a slot on Channel 4 the following year, as he and Mortimer rented a back room at Jools Holland's office/recording studio in Westcombe Park, Greenwich where they'd spend hours writing material.

Moir chose the stage name Reeves because of his fondness for the American singer Jim Reeves. He continued to work alongside Mortimer as a comedy duo in The Smell of Reeves and Mortimer, Shooting Stars, and 'Bang Bang, It's Reeves and Mortimer', some of which also featured future cast members of The Fast Show and Little Britain.

James is one of the few comedians to have had a UK chart-topping single, with The Wonder Stuff, singing 'Dizzy', previously a # 1 for Tommy Roe. Moir also released two other singles from his album I Will Cure You (1991). A pilot programme written by Paul Whitehouse and Charlie Higson during 1994, entitled The Honeymoon's Over, was due to feature Chris Bell, a character from The Smell of Reeves and Mortimer but the series was never commissioned. That same year, Vic made a guest appearance on the Radio 1 series Shuttleworth's Showtime, hosted by John Shuttleworth.

James and Bob presented the Channel X produced BBC Saturday game show 'Families at War' with Alice Beer from August 1998 and May 1999. Moir played Marty Hopkirk in the BBC's thriller series Randall and Hopkirk (Deceased) between 2000–2001—a revival of the original series from the 1960s, with Mortimer as Randall, Emilia Fox as Jeannie and Tom Baker as Wyvern.

James presented a series entitled, Vic Reeves Examines on UK Play in the year 2000, featuring celebrities including Ricky Gervais, Johnny Vegas, Lauren Laverne and Emma Kennedy discussing a topic of their choice. That same year, Moir presented a one-off radio show on BBC Radio 1, entitled Cock of the Wood. Reeves appeared on the BBC Radio programme Desert Island Discs during 2003.

James and his 2nd wife, Nancy Sorrell were both contestants on the 4th series of I'm a Celebrity... Get Me Out of Here! the following year. Moir was then featured in the series Catterick with Mortimer, appearing as several characters. He hosted a show for Virgin Radio in September 2005, titled Vic Reeves Big Night In, produced by Mark Augustyn, for a short period on Wednesdays & Thursdays from 7.00pm.

James presented a programme on ITV Tyne Tees during May the following year, about Northeast comedy culture, named It's Funny Up North with... Vic Reeves. Moir presented an historical

10-part series, entitled Rogues Gallery, shown on the Discovery Channel (UK) in 2005, in which he investigated, and portrayed Anne Bonny, Mary Read, Captain Kidd, Claude Duval, Jonathan Wild, Rob Roy, Colonel Blood, George Ransley, Deacon Brodie, Blackbeard and Dick Turpin, Nancy Sorrell appearing in some episodes. Vic Reeves' Pirates was shown on ITV West then on the History Channel during 2007.

James also hosted a show titled 'Vic Reeves Investigates: Jack the Ripper', in which he tried to discover who Jack the Ripper was, with the help of historians and leading experts. At the end of the show, Moir came to the conclusion that Jack the Ripper was Francis Tumblety. Vic was the main presenter of Brainiac: Science Abuse from 8th May 2007, during the 5th & 6th series, replacing Richard Hammond. Reeves presented a BBC Radio 2 panel game show titled Does the Team Think? from June that year.

James appeared in a weekly sketch show on BBC Radio 2 from 17th November 2007, entitled Vic Reeves' House Arrest. The show's premise was that Moir had been put under house arrest for 'a crime he didn't commit', each episode being comprised of the events that took place in and around his house on a particular day. Bob played his housecall-making hairdresser, Carl, while other performers included The Mighty Boosh star Noel Fielding as a local vagrant who came to Vic's door on a weekly basis looking for work, as well as Sorrell in multiple roles.

James announced on 27th February 2008 that he and Mortimer were working together on a new sitcom about super heroes who got their powers via a malfunctioning telegraph pole, having also reiterated his desire to bring back Shooting Stars for a 6th series. Along with his son, Reeves was also featured an edition of a factual series for Five, Dangerous Adventures for Boys, based on the best-selling book of that name by Conn and Hal Iggulden.

Moir appeared as presenter of the first episode of My Brilliant Britain in February 2009, one of the new shows commissioned for UKTV People channel's relaunch as Blighty. Vic appeared as a guest on the BBC One's The One Show with Bob on 25th August 2009, the day before Series 6 of Shooting Stars began, featuring James and Mortimer, along with Ulrika Jonsson and Jack Dee as team captains.

Reeves appeared as one of the guests in Reece Shearsmith's Haunted House that autumn, a light-hearted radio discussion show broadcast on BBC Radio 4 in two parts either side of Halloween, on 29th October then 5th November. Moir also voiced a Virgin Atlantic Airlines onboard safety video, with Dani Behr. Vic & Bob performed a selection of YouTube improvised comedy sketches during July 2011, in association with Foster's, posting their 'Afternoon Delight' clips every weekday afternoon that month.

James has appeared without Mortimer on a number of British TV shows, mainly game shows, poll programmes and charity telethons, including:

Year(s)	Title	Channel	Role	No. of episodes	Notes
2017	Coronation Street	ITV	Colin Callen	7+	Credited as Jim Moir
2017	Celebrity Masterchef	BBC 1	Contestant		

2015   Catchphrase: Celebrity Couples Special   ITV   Contestant   1

With Bob Mortimer

Celebrity Benchmark   Channel 4   Benchmarker/contestant

Celebrity Fifteen to One Channel 4   Contestant   1

Room 101   BBC 1   1

Inspector George Gently   BBC 1   Geoffrey   Episode 7.3 'Gently Among Friends'   credited as Jim Moir

2014

Tipping Point: Lucky Stars   ITV   Contestant   1   Won   credited as Jim Moir

Racing Legends: Barry Sheene   BBC 2   Presenter   1

credited as Jim Moir

2013

Big Star's Little Star   ITV Contestant   1   with daughters Nell and Lizzie (2nd October), credited as Jim Moir

2013

Great British Menu   BBC 2   Guest judge   1   credited as Jim Moir

2012

Hebburn   BBC 2   Joe Pearson   5   credited as Jim Moir

2012

The Million Pound Drop Channel 4   Contestant – with Bob Mortimer   1

credited as Jim Moir

2012

The Ministry of Curious Stuff   CBBC   Presenter (with Dan Skinner)   13

credited as Jim Moir

2011

Vic Reeves' Turner Prize Moments   Channel 4   Presenter   1

The Fun Police   Channel 4   Richard Traves   1   Pilot
credited as Jim Moir

Eric and Ernie   BBC 2   George Bartholomew, father of Eric Morecambe   1

credited as Jim Moir

2010

Never Mind The Buzzcocks   BBC 2   Panelist – on Noel Fielding's team   1

Series 24   Episode 9

2009

My Brilliant Britain   Blighty   presenter   1   2008

Show	Channel	Role	#
Celebrity Come Dine With Me	Channel 4	waiter / support for contestant Nancy Sorrell	1
Dangerous Adventures For Boys	Five	Contestant (with son, Louis Moir)	1
Hole in the Wall	BBC 1	Contestant (with Nancy Sorrell)	1
The Culture Show Uncut	BBC 2	Reporter	1
Take It Or Leave It (with Nancy Sorrell)	Challenge	Celebrity contestant	1
2008 BRIT Awards	ITV	Award presenter	

2007–2008

| Would I Lie To You? | BBC 1 | Panel member | 2 |

2005–2008

| 8 Out of 10 Cats | Channel 4 | Panel member | 8 |

2007

Loose Women	ITV	Interviewee (with Nancy Sorrell)	1
The One Show	BBC 1	Interviewee	1
Something for the Weekend	BBC 2	Interviewee	1
Deadline	ITV2	Contestant (with Nancy Sorrell)	1
Memoirs of a Cigarette	Channel 4	Contributor	1

Vic Reeves' Pirates	HTV the History Channel	Presenter	6
Vic Reeves Investigates: Jack the Ripper	Sky One	Presenter	
Pirate Ship... Live	Five	Presenter	
The Big Fat Anniversary Quiz	Channel 4	Guest appearance	
Brainiac: Science Abuse	Sky One	Presenter	21 Series 5 & 6
Shaun the Sheep	CBBC BBC 1	Theme tune 'Shaun the Sheep – Life's a Treat'	
Vernon Kay's Gameshow Marathon	ITV1	Panel member	1 Blankety Blank episode
100 Greatest Stand Ups	Channel 4	Contributor	
The Grumpy Guide to... Art	BBC 2	Contributor	Spinoff of Grumpy Old Men
Dale's Supermarket Sweep	ITV1	Contestant	1
Law of the Playground	Channel 4	Contributor	11
The Truth About Food	BBC 2	Contributor	

2006–2007

QI	BBC 2	Panel member	4

1998–2007

Never Mind the Buzzcocks BBC 2 Panel member 2

2006

Turn Back Time BBC 2 Interviewee 1

It's Funny Up North with... Vic Reeves Tyne Tees ITV1 Presenter

The Story of Light Entertainment BBC 2 Contributor 2

Summer Exhibition BBC 2 Panel judge

Comedy Connections – 'Shooting Stars' BBC 1 /Subject / Interviewee 1

Jools Holland's Hootenanny BBC 2 Interviewee singer

2004–2006

Richard & Judy Channel 4 Interviewee 3

2002–2006

Friday Night with Jonathan Ross BBC 1 Interviewee 2

2005

The South Bank Show ITV1 Subject / Interviewee 1

The Best & Worst of God BBC 2 Presenter

Final Chance to Save Sky One Contributor

Rogues Gallery Discovery Channel UK Presenter 10

10

The Death of Celebrity	Channel 4	Contributor
50 Greatest Comedy Sketches	Channel 4	Contributor

2004

I'm a Celebrity... Get Me Out of Here!	ITV1	Contestant (with Nancy Sorrell) 8
Who Do You Think You Are?	BBC 2	Subject 1
Star Sale	BBC 1	Contributor 1
Hell's Kitchen	ITV1	Boorish Customer 1
Breakfast	BBC 1	Interviewee 1
Vic's Chicks	BBC 3	Presenter 10 via the red button

2003

Auction Man	BBC 1	
Most Haunted	Living TV	Celebrity guest (with Nancy Sorrell) 1

2002

Celebrity Mastermind	BBC 2	Contestant 1 Reeves' specialist subject was 'Pirates'
Surrealissimo – The Trial of Salvador Dalí	BBC 2	
BBC Four	Paul Éluard	

These Things Take Time – The Story of the Smiths
ITV1	Narrator

2001

It's Your New Year's Eve Party	BBC 1	Contributor

British Comedy Awards 2001	ITV1	Award presenter

I Love the '90s	BBC 2	Contributor	1	'I Love 1991' episode

We Know Where You Live. Live!	Channel 4	Performer	Four Yorkshiremen sketch

Comic Relief: Say Pants to Poverty	BBC 1	Presenter

Top Ten	Channel 4	Contributor	1	'Prog Rock' episode

2000

Vic Reeves Examines	Play UK	Presenter	12

Randall & Hopkirk (Deceased)	BBC 1	Marty Hopkirk	13

Robot Wars	BBC 2	Contestant

Night of a Thousand Shows	BBC 1

Dale's All Stars	BBC 1	Interviewee	1

This Is Your Life Episode for Tom Baker	BBC 1	Contributor	1

1999

Clive Anderson All Talk	Channel 4	Interviewee	1

1996

TFI Friday	Channel 4	Interviewee	2

1995

Children in Need	BBC 1	Contributor

1993

British Comedy Awards 1993	ITV

Moir is a serious artist, as well as a comedian, although the two often combine, his works including paintings, ceramics, photographs and lino prints, being in a distinctive style. His work has been described as Dada-esque, surreal and sometimes macabre, his art and comedy having become different ways of expressing the same idea, James saying "I think putting your imagination on canvas or a television screen is the same thing, I don't differentiate between painting, acting or comedy. I think everything I do is art." Reeves has stated that he's an artist 1st, a comedian 2nd, hoping that he'll be remembered for his art and writing in 10 years' time, rather than his comedy.

Much like his comedy, Vic isn't one to analyse his artworks, having said that art should be "just for laughs", disliking folk looking for statements in his work, because there are none. "If something makes me laugh, that's it. I've done straight drawings and paintings ... but I haven't got as much pleasure out of them as if I'd done something that'd make me laugh". His work was described by artists Jake and Dinos Chapman as 'able to command our laughter as a purgative, to encourage the viewer to leak at both ends', artist Damien Hirst, a friend of Moir, having also described him as an influence.

The crossover of comedy and art often features within James & Bob's TV shows, as in The Smell of Reeves and Mortimer's first episode, in which several of Vic's drawings were featured, illustrating the lyrics of the opening song, later being published in his book 'Sun Boiled Onions'. As in the script book for the show, Moir often drew sketches for the BBC's costume and set designers saying that "if we just tell them what we want, it never ends up looking like it does in our minds".

Arts and crafts played a large part in James's upbringing, his mother, a seamstress, and father, a typesetter, made extra money by selling handmade wooden crafts and ceramics at local markets. Reeves began charging for his artistic services, including customising and painting his friend's school bags and elaborately embroidering clothing, later producing artworks his acquaintances liked, hoping that they'd buy them. Wanting to study art, but being pressured into getting a job, Vic began a 5-year engineering apprenticeship at a factory in Newton Aycliffe with the aim of working in their technical drawings department.

After completing the apprenticeship, Moir applied to Goldsmith's College in London to study art, failing to get a place but sneaking in to use their equipment. He completed a one-year foundation course at Sir John Cass College in 1983, where

James later became an honorary graduate. Once leaving college, he worked as a curator at the independent Garden Gallery in London, where he held his first art exhibition during 1985, with the help of a grant from Lewisham Council.

He's published two books of his art, Sun Boiled Onions (1999), followed by 'Vic Reeves' Vast Book of World Knowledge', in 2009. His drawings were also included in his autobiography Me:Moir Volume One, along with the published script book for The Smell of Reeves and Mortimer. He provided 30 illustrations for Random House's reprint of Jerome K. Jerome's classic story 'Three Men in a Boat' (2011). James was also commissioned to create several celebrity drawings for Jools Holland's Channel 5 series Name That Tune.

Vic has hosted several exhibitions of his artwork, including:

Sun Boiled Onions (2000) at the Percy Miller Gallery

Doings (2002) at the Whitechapel Gallery, London

My Family and Other Freaks (2007) at the Eyestorm Gallery, London

Where Eagles Tremble (2009) at Mews of Mayfair, London

Hot Valve Leak: Visual Ramblings of Vic Reeves (2013) at the Strand Gallery, London

A selection of Moir's paintings were displayed at the Saatchi Gallery, London during 2010, as part of an exhibition by charity 'The Art of Giving'. He was also a judge for the charity's open art competition.

James took part in the Illuminating York festival during 2012, his illuminations, named 'Wonderland', being projected across a number of historic buildings including the Yorkshire Museum, St Mary's Abbey, and the 10-acre site of York Museum Gardens.

Before becoming famous as a comedian, Reeves was a member of several bands with many different names and musical styles, in which he usually played bass guitar and/or sang. Vic sold tapes of his early material in the back pages of NME magazine under the name 'International Cod'. Mark Lamarr, later to become a team captain in Shooting Stars, was sent a tape of Moir's group 'Fan Tan Tiddly Span'. When James appeared on Never Mind the Buzzcocks in 1998, Lamarr repeatedly played a sample from the song 'Fantasia (Side A)' to embarrass him.

As part of early Big Night Out performances, Reeves would sometimes hand out promotional materials to the audience. On one occasion he handed out a 7" flexi disc of original song 'The Howlin' Wind'. Having surplus copies of the discs, Vic passed them on to Darlington-based band Dan who then included a copy of the disc with their L.P. Kicking Ass at T.J.'s.

'I Will Cure You', Moir's only album, was issued during 1991 by Island Records, hitting UK No. 16, having featured the chart-topping single 'Dizzy', which was a collaboration with The Wonder Stuff. It included a mixture of covers and original songs in a variety of musical styles, many of which were originally introduced in Big Night Out. A couple of other singles were also released from the L.P., a cover of the Matt Monro song 'Born Free' and a dance reworking of Christian hymn Abide With Me, which reached No. 6 and No. 47 in the UK Singles Chart, respectively.

James and Bob issued a cover of The Monkees song 'I'm a Believer' with British group EMF in 1995, which hit UK No. 3, Reeves having previously sung the track at the beginning of early Big Night Out performances in London, and opened the Channel 4 series with it. In the music video, which Vic directed, the duo dressed as Mike Nesmith and Davy Jones of The Monkees. On the CD release of the single, a studio version of 'At This Stage I Couldn't Say' was included, a track originally sung by characters Mulligan and O'Hare in The Smell of Reeves and Mortimer. On the 7" issue, the bonus track was 'At Least We've Got Our Guitars', which was the opening song for the last episode of The Smell of Reeves and Mortimer.

The theme to British stop-motion animation Shaun the Sheep, sung by Moir, was released as a single during April 2007, the song making UK No. 20. Reeves and Mortimer contributed backing vocals to Jools Holland's 'Holy Cow', a Lee Dorsey cover in 1990, the track being included on Holland's album World of his Own and also issued as a single. James later advertised Holland's L.P. Moving Out to the Country.

Vic provided backing vocals for Morrissey's cover of 'That's Entertainment' that year, originally by The Jam, his vocals not being used in the final edit but he was thanked (as Jim Moir) in the sleeve notes of Morrissey's 'Sing Your Life' single, which featured 'That's Entertainment' as a bonus track. A fan of the Smiths, Reeves opened some episodes of Big Night Out with covers of the band's songs, including 'Sheila Take a Bow', which he intended to include a cover of on his album I Will Cure You but it didn't make the final cut.

James contributed a track to Ruby Trax (1992), a compilation L.P. released by NME magazine to commemorate 40 years of the publication, having covered the Ultravox song 'Vienna', but drastically altered the original lyrics. Vic contributed to Twentieth-Century Blues: The Songs of Noel Coward (1998), a tribute album featuring artists including Elton John, Sting, Robbie Williams and Paul McCartney. Moir covered Coward's track 'Don't Put Your Daughter on the Stage Mrs. Worthington' (1934), which was arranged by David Arnold for the L.P. The song, described by Reeves as 'sinister', was initially recorded with all original verses intact, but as the last included foul language, it was edited out of the final issue.

James's cover of 'Ain't That a Kick in the Head?' was featured during the year 2000 as a bonus track on the theme single to the Randall and Hopkirk (Deceased) series in which he starred. Vic was originally due to duet with Nina Persson of the Cardigans, who provided vocals, but missed the final cut. A shortened version of Moir's cover also featured in the series, Reeves and Mortimer appearing in the music video for the single.

Jim has also appeared in music videos for other artists, his first having been that for Shakin' Stevens' single 'What Do You Want to Make Those Eyes at Me For (1987), being hired for the shoot for £10. Vic was also in the music video for Band of Holy Joy's song 'Tactless', the following year, introducing the group then appearing at the bar part way through. The video was filmed in Deptford, London, with original advertising posters for Big Night Out being seen at the beginning.

Vic Reeves' Vast Book of World Knowledge – a surreal encyclopaedia with text and artwork by Reeves. Atlantic Books, was published in October 2009. It followed Vic Reeves Me:Moir

(Volume One) – autobiography by Vic Reeves, Virgin Books, 2006 & Sunboiled Onions – diary, paintings and drawings by Vic Reeves, Penguin Books, 1999

James has appeared in TV adverts, both with Bob and alone, one for Guinness quoting Moir as saying "88.2% of statistics are made up on the spot". Vic has featured in solo advertising work for a variety of products including MFI, Müller Light, First Direct, Churchill Insurance, Cadbury's Boost, Mars Bar, Fanta, Heinz Tomato Ketchup, Domestos bleach and Maryland Cookies, having cross-dressed for an advert for 888 Holdings' Bingo website 888 Ladies in 2008.

Jim also advertised Jools Holland's album Moving Out to the Country during 2006. Reeves was in an East Coast Trains TV advert to promote the first-class service in 2011, having sketched then painted passengers and an attendant. Moir was also in a radio advert for the company the following year.

James Roderick Moir is the son of James Neill (1926–2004) and Audrey Moir (née Leigh). He moved from Leeds to Darlington, County Durham when 5 years old, with his parents and younger sister Lois. Jim attended Heathfield Infants and Junior School then went on to the nearby secondary school, Eastbourne Comprehensive in Darlington.

Vic has 4 children, the eldest two by his first wife Sarah Vincent, whom he wed during 1990 then divorced in 1999. He met his 2nd wife, Nancy Sorrell, during 2001, the couple marrying on 25th January 2003. Nancy gave birth to twin girls Beth and Nell at the William Harvey Hospital in Ashford, Kent, on 25th May 2006. Reeves lives in Charing, near Ashford, where he buried his classic Austin A40 Somerset car in his back garden, as shown on the Omnibus documentary 'A Film of Reeves & Mortimer', shown on the BBC during 1997. James & Bob are lifelong fans of the rock band Free.

"I came up with the Vic Reeves character for a stage project, folk presume that's my name, even when I do other acting jobs. I've been trying to shake it off for about 20 years. Vic started off as an overblown northern club compere, then slowly evolved into a complete idiot.

The first thing I remember – and this has been qualified by my mother – is being in a pram. She left me outside a shop and I remember seeing corrugated iron above me, so I was probably quite disturbed that she'd abandoned me. I also remember a kid called John Boxer, who locked me in his toy box.

My playground growing up was the fields and forests. I had a brief stint in London in my 20s, but I live in the country again now. I go walking and birdwatching. I've just finished a documentary about video arts, one of the films including a lot of wading birds on an estuary. I could name them all.

I've been accident-prone since I was a kid climbing trees and falling out. I've come off a few motorcycles. A few years ago, I went under a tractor. I've been under a lorry. The last time, I had a huge bruise on my left buttock, like a black plate, so I had to sit in a peculiar position. I tried to keep it quiet, but it was spotted one morning when I got out of bed.

Painting is my chief passion. I've always done it. I've just put a bit more effort into it over the past 10 years. It pays more money than other work for a start. I've got notebooks all round the house and I go into my studio at the end of my garden virtually every day. I'm still lively, 60 is like 40 now, isn't it? I've just finished a Big Night Out and I was leaping off the desk. I got famous in my 20s, so I kind of stick at that age.

I've got a 26-year-old, a 22-year-old and two 13-year-olds. The twins think I'm some ancient megalith. What I really like doing is surprising them by secretly studying things that make me look cool, like learning the Fortnite dance. I cook every day and find it really relaxing. I've got a huge number of cookery books. It's usually traditional British and French cooking, but then I'll go off-piste. I've just been doing Ainsley Harriott's Caribbean.

There's a lot to be depressed about, so I try to avoid doing it. The constantly hot summers are a bit of a worry and plastic. We were at a fish and chip restaurant recently, where they had sachets of vinegar. I found myself being a grumpy old man: "Look at all this plastic, why don't you just have the vinegar in a bottle?" I don't say it publicly, I just do my own private mithering. After my early youth of thinking isn't socialism fantastic, I let life pass by.

Vic and Bob were bringing their Big Night Out back to the BBC. The Christmas special, which was followed by a 4-part series, included a jaunty song about trousers, a skit on First Dates, a punch-up, Ed Sheeran, some 'observation comedy' and a baker from Wisconsin selling 'perfuffle' cakes. You should see the stuff that didn't make the edit, said Reeves. "There were some spectacular moments, like when we tried to get a horse on the stage". A horse? "We wanted to look under it and see what was going on, but the horse was a bit frisky. He wouldn't go on". Mortimer gestured at the BBC Comedy offices opposite. "You'd think there'd be someone out there who deals with horses".

It was 30 years since Jim Moir and Bob Mortimer teamed up, so when the BBC asked them for a one-off special, they'd decided to go back to their roots. Their first TV show, Vic Reeves' Big Night Out, a surreal spoof of a variety show, debuted on Channel 4 in 1990. James was Vic Reeves, the flamboyantly controlling compere; Bob was his sidekick, playing all manner of roles from The Man with the Stick to Morrissey the consumer monkey.

Vic and Bob's Big Night Out brought back some of that show's key elements - grumpy Graham Lister, bizarro talent segment, Novelty Island then the closing song, mixing it with a dash of The Smell of Reeves and Mortimer, along with a hint of Shooting Stars. Basically, it was half an hour of peculiar sketches, wigs, bickering and unsettling props. "Everyone's a one-trick pony aren't they?" said Bob. "It always ends up being the same ballpark. We've only ever done what we like. We do what we enjoy doing, because then it looks like you're enjoying yourself. We are enjoying ourselves", said Moir.

When they were writing, Mortimer drove from his house in Tunbridge Wells to Jim's near Ashford for 9.30am then they worked through until 2pm. "Just talking and shouting. We'll say, 'what shall we write a song about? Blackberries? Chinese parrots?' Then Jim says 'trousers' and we both laugh our heads off. Learn your lines, no autocue, no retakes. Just 3, 2, 1, go. It feels like a nice challenge. If you really, really are funny, you've got 30 minutes", said Bob.

When they shot the original Big Night Out, their scripts were 3 pages long, they wouldn't let the cameramen see them in advance, shooting the whole show in 30 minutes. "We got into trouble for it. We're not telly people. We didn't know the rules and naively we wanted everyone - the cameramen and so on - to laugh when they heard it on the night. We genuinely didn't want to give the jokes away," said Mortimer.

They wanted the new show to feel as immediate as in the old days, so they filmed it at the intimate Hospital Club in London, having hired Mat Whitecross, known for music documentaries including Oasis: Supersonic, "to shoot it live, like a pop concert". It took 50 mins from start to finish, whereas most TV comedy shows take hours. "It's dreary, innit. We guess that we're the only ones stupid enough, who have the balls? The balls, Jim?" asked Bob. "The gusto", corrected Vic. "The gusto, to do an underwritten show - go out in front of an audience and just film it. Learn your lines, no autocue, no retakes. Just 3, 2, 1, go. It feels like a nice challenge. If you really, really are funny, you've got 30 minutes".

It was an ethos that had served them well so far. Ever since Mortimer, then a solicitor, was one of 7 audience members at a comedy night in the Goldsmiths Tavern in New Cross, where he watched Reeves tap-dance in a Bryan Ferry mask with planks tied to his feet. A couple of weeks later, Moir got Bob up on stage then presented him with a giant cheque for £8m made out to 'ill kids'. They started writing together the next day.

Their success was stellar - their audience doubling by the week. "If you were going to see Jim, you were going back next week, but taking someone with you" said Bob. The show went from the room above the pub to the room downstairs, to the Albany Empire, where they were spotted by Alan Yentob and Michael Grade, who put them on Channel 4.

"The comedy circuit kind of resented us, because they were slogging away. We never fitted in anywhere - not by design, that's just what we thought was funny. We've never copied anyone else. Originally from having a lack of knowledge about what comics do then realising, we're onto a winner here, because no-one's doing anything like this. Now there are a lot of young lasses and lads and they're quite intense - there isn't that joy. They want to get on telly and on panel shows. Our motivation came from having a laugh. We're the only double act that is left," said Vic. Ant and Dec? "They're more like presenters. They just read off an autocue and someone writes it all". Mitchell and Webb? "They're just actors in some sketches. We've written and learned then we veer off. There's no-one at all doing that", said James.

The key to their success, said Mortimer, was that they got into comedy to have fun, rather than a career. "It was just a way of us having a nice night out. The route for two blokes in a pub in Deptford to being on telly didn't exist - maybe for Oxbridge types, but that wasn't the end game. "What do modern comedians do? Do they just tell long, rambling stories? And you occasionally get a laugh?" said Reeves. "It's the weirdest thing, Vic. I'm seeing some famous comics now who want to be gurus," marveled Bob.

They had absolutely zero interest in incorporating a message, or even a nod to current affairs, in their comedy. "I've never in my life met anyone as apolitical as Jim. I seem to remember on the day of the Brexit vote you weren't aware of it. I asked how you voted and you were like, 'What for?' It's not a bad place to be, really. We come from the school of if you're going to do comedy, we want to cram as many laughs as we can. One every 5 mins wouldn't do me. We want one every 5 secs", said Mortimer. "I'm only interested in fine art. We'd never put anything political in what we do, because I don't think it's the right thing to do", said Moir.

That was the rationale behind their bonkers sitcom House of Fools, which was axed by the BBC after two seasons during 2015. "We thought it was fabulous", said Bob. "We thought it was the pinnacle. We tried to get as many laughs in as possible. I think we probably would be in the Guinness Book of Records for the amount of laughs in a sitcom. The BBC say, 'It's got to have warmth, there's got to be a narrative, there's got to be a character like this, an enemy. We kind of ignored that and thought - surely five people can just say funny lines for 24 minutes. We had a bit of a story - there'd be a big moth attacking the town, or something. There aren't any decent sitcoms on now. I can't think of any," said James.

The pair went back on the road in 2016 for the first time in almost two decades. The tour was postponed for 3 months when Mortimer went for a routine check-up, discovering that his arteries were 95% blocked. He was booked in for a triple heart bypass 4 days later. On the morning of the operation, he thought he might die, so wed his long-term partner, Lisa, with whom he has two sons, aged 19 and 20.

Bob said he was fine now, being a lot less worried than he was soon after the operation when he lived off a diet of seeds. "Has your food regime changed? When we were on tour, he refused a pork pie from Melton Mowbray, which I thought was ridiculous. Would you have a pork pie now?" asked Reeves. "I eat all sorts of sh*t, Jim and you just feel bad. For people who've had heart operations, it's very difficult at the moment because half of science believes you shouldn't eat any saturated fat and half of science believes you should eat as much as you can. So you eat a cake, then you eat a statin, and think, 'that will work'", said Mortimer.

"You could do a modern stand-up routine about it," said Vic. "Yes, I'd go on at Edinburgh with me heart story. It'd all build up to me eating a pork pie on stage and everyone would be standing up, clapping, saying, 'yes that's rather clever'", said Bob. It was, said Moir, a shock to see his comedy partner so ill, having started getting chest pains in sympathy, patting his chest. "It's psychosomatic but you think, 'Oh God'. You get to a certain age…"

That week he'd been worried that he had emphysema. "I was a bit short of breath but then I found quite a lot of people had the same chest infection". He'd begun swimming half a mile / day, after dropping his daughters off at school. "I go early so there's me and a lot of old ladies. Old ladies everywhere". At the age of 58, did they worry about doing what they do and getting older? "Physically, yes, but we're still very spritely. I notice it when we're still writing things that would suggest we're about 30. We should be writing about widows, not 'Ooh I've got a new girlfriend'", said James.

Their reunion tour had been more sedate than their previous one during the '90s, when they'd drunk all night after shows - "ending up in some club in Liverpool then some council estate in Manchester…", said Mortimer. These days, they'd have a pint of the local real ale then go to bed. They didn't socialise as much as they'd used to, either, when they'd seen each other every night, gone on holiday together. "It's that family thing, you retreat to your house," said Bob. "I like making dinner and watching the telly," agreed Vic, who had 11-year old twins with his 2nd wife Nancy Sorrell and two older children from his first marriage.

In recent years, they'd worked on solo projects, Mortimer's surreal football podcast Athletico Mince having amassed over 7 million listens. Reeves painted most days in the huge studio that he'd built at home - he'd recently been creating screenprints of the original Big Night Out paintings. "Noel Fielding bought two of my paintings the other day," he said. "They're beautiful, Jim's paintings," said Bob, who had a painting Moir had done of him on his hospital bed with a heart pinned to his chest, with another of a large fluffy elephant. "You can keep that one", said James.

Thirty years on, their instinct was still - if it makes them laugh, it works. "If we make each other laugh then everyone else laughs," said Vic. "I went to a comedy show recently, which wasn't particularly funny but he was very engaging. I had this terrible feeling that his end game was to make people think, 'He's a thoughtful, clever bloke isn't he?' My hope is that people leave saying, 'that was funny, that was'", said Mortimer. "Or 'Those two are proper idiots. Pair of morons. Are they really that thick?'" agreed Reeves. "'They're complete f*cking idiots,'" said Bob, happily. "That's such a compliment". Strange fella...

'Have you ever damaged your phone in unusual circumstances? e.g: It's fallen on a very hard lizard or it's melted during prayer,' asked Mortimer. It turned out that Jim said there was an anal-based incident on a ridge which fitted the bill. Thereafter, further lines of questioning included: "Is it inappropriate to have a comforting funeral candle scented with bubblegum? On a cross-Channel ferry do you mainly stare at the funnel or the railings? Have you ever rented out a room for men to sleep? Have you ever been to Peterborough - on your own? Do you wish that Sports Direct sold food as well?

To that last question Moir replied "I'd love to have a sneaker which has an interior compartment, which contains hummus or taramasalata or any of the Greek dips". At a preview event in London to mark the return of their show to BBC Four, there was some insight into the pair's career of over 35-years, as they shared archive pictures – as well as some indiscreet celebrity gossip.

James recalled a certain future Britain's Got Talent judge loitering on set while they were shooting their sketches. "He used to hang around everywhere. You'd look in the corner and there was Walliams. It's because we got Matt Lucas on when he was 17, who said 'Can I bring my mate along?' He used to hang around in corners. One time – and I do remember this – when we were doing Randall & Hopkirk, we filmed a scene for an hour and a half then all of a sudden Walliams came out of a wardrobe. He'd been hiding in there. Very strange fella". "There's some truth in that," Bob added.

After being shown a photo of himself in Jools Holland's office in Greenwich, South London, where they used to write Big Night Out, Mortimer recalled: "We had an English Gentlemen's

Motorcycle club. You had to have an English motorcycle and dress like an English gentleman. Paul Young, the singer of 'Wherever I Lay My Hat', asked if he could join. He came in wearing those leather trousers with tassels all down the side". He drove a Harley-Davidson,' Vic added.

Bob continued: "Me, you and Jools went into a room while he waited outside – we decided he couldn't join". Reeves stated that they based their rules on the Hell's Angels initiation ceremony in which new members had to bite the head off a chicken: "Our rules were that you had to present a chicken dinner to every guest. Also, whenever you pass a lady you raise your helmet".

Mortimer recalled rather a bruising first encounter with the acting legend Derek Jacobi. "We were doing Randall and Hopkirk, I hadn't met met him. He was called something like let's say, Professor Whittingshield. They went, 'Action!' I said, 'Hello, Professor Whislingshield', getting it wrong. He went, 'Oh you c*nt!' – with the word intoned violently". Vic also recalled a scene from the same episode, when a hefty guard had to punch Bob, who was supposed to move out of the way but he didn't, so the actor knocked him unconscious 'For about 5 minutes'.

Reeves recalled a gruelling shoot with the former Dr Who in a studio that was a roasting 140F. "It was ridiculous, but Tom said, 'Jim at the end of this I'm going to make a Tom Baker Special'". Which turned out to be a gin and tonic or rather "It was a bucket full of gin and he threw a lemon in it. We actually drank it". The pair lived relatively close to each other in Kent, so Moir, a regular house guest, later bought Baker's house off him, although he didn't disclose whether it was bigger on the inside... Next to it was a churchyard, James recalling: "He already had his grave there, which said 'Tom Baker 1934-' ... but with no end date. He's the greatest bloke".

The audience at the event at the British Film Institute were shown several photos from Vic's own archive, including an early incarnation of the oddly attired character Tom Fun. "I'm going to say this is 1992. Those were fantastic days of wardrobe, with make-up staff who'd say, 'We don't know what you want to do, and you obviously don't, here's a big bag of stuff' then we'd come out looking like that developing the characters from that".

Another pic showed Moir on stage at the Regent's Park Open Air Theatre in London, with a badly-made puppet having the face of Nick Kamen, the model who was famous for a steamy ad for Levi's jeans set in a launderette in 1985. James recalled: "These puppets were made by me. As you can tell, not by an expert. This is long before the Big Night Out went on TV. I got commissioned – commissioned!

I got asked to do a concert in Regent's Park with Suzanne Vega. I turned up but they were horrible people. Suzanne Vega and all her crew were having a nice dinner. I came along then said 'I'm the warm-up turn'. They took me to what was pretty much a woodshed that had shovels in it, told me to wait. I said, 'Can I have a drink?' Someone gave me a can of lager when all the others were having this nice food". It was no better when Vic got to the stage, "They thought I was going to be a stand-up but it was a lot more than that. No one liked it; everyone hated every single moment".

That opinion was also shared by some reviewers, the pair sharing a write-up they received of a night in Malcolm Hardee's notorious Tunnel Club during the '80s, which described them as 'riotously unfunny'. It sarcastically described a sketch in which 'the area's least-gifted crab gave a lecture on the forests of Scotland. The audience was deeply impressed by this, clamouring for the next act but the Walker Brothers turned out to be pantomime bears leaping around to music. Their antics included a simulated sex act'.

Another picture showed Reeves as Tappy Lappy, a very early character from the days he performed Big Night Out at Goldsmiths Tavern in South London. Moir and his pal Johnny Irvine had cut out portraits of Bryan Ferry from the front of Face magazine, having taped them to their own heads, preempting the cardboard face masks that appeared in joke shops everywhere.

"Bob turned up that night to see Tappy Lappy. We sellotaped wooden planks to our feet, having had tap dancing sound effects made by dropping cutlery and cans in our house. Turning to his friend, he said: 'You saw that then thought, 'I want to be part of that'. Then Bob said: 'You'll never know, Jim'. It was amazing to come to that as a stranger and know there was nothing like that in the world". Thirty-five years on, there still wasn't...

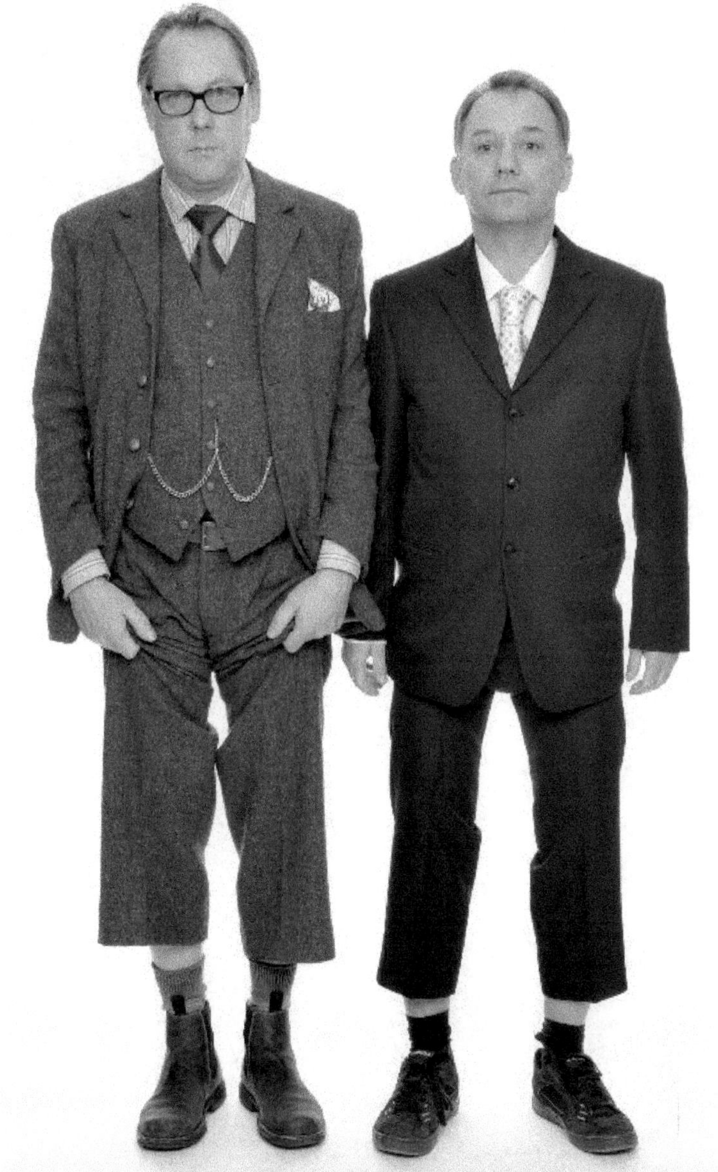

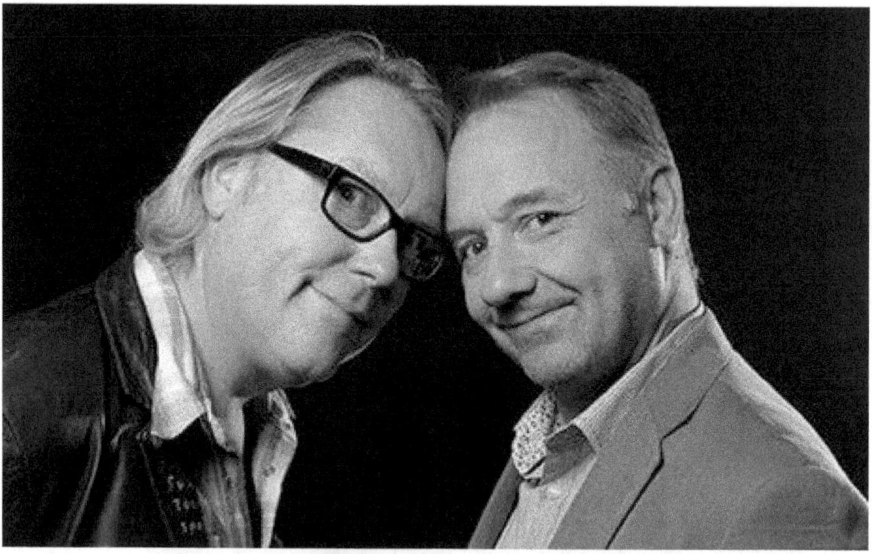

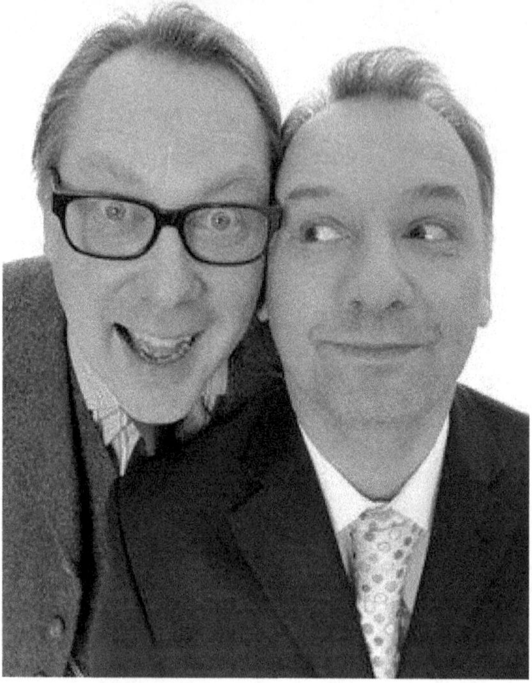

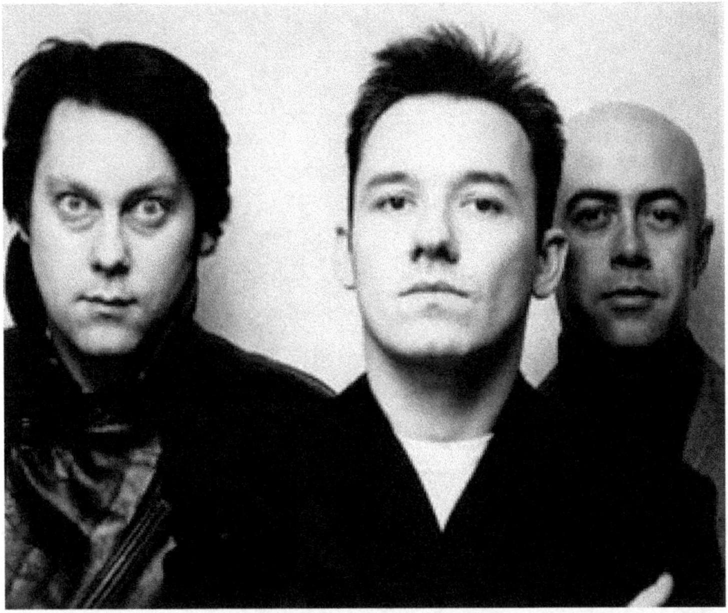

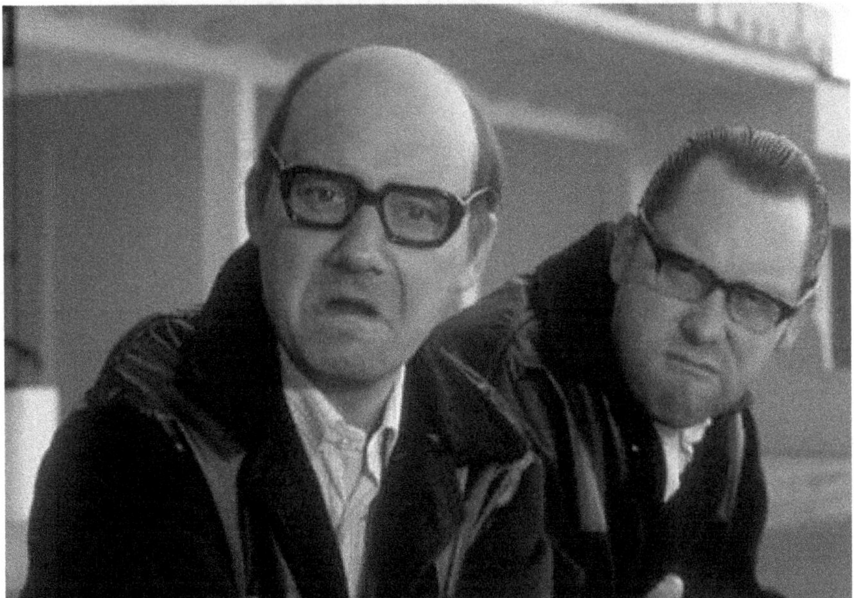

39

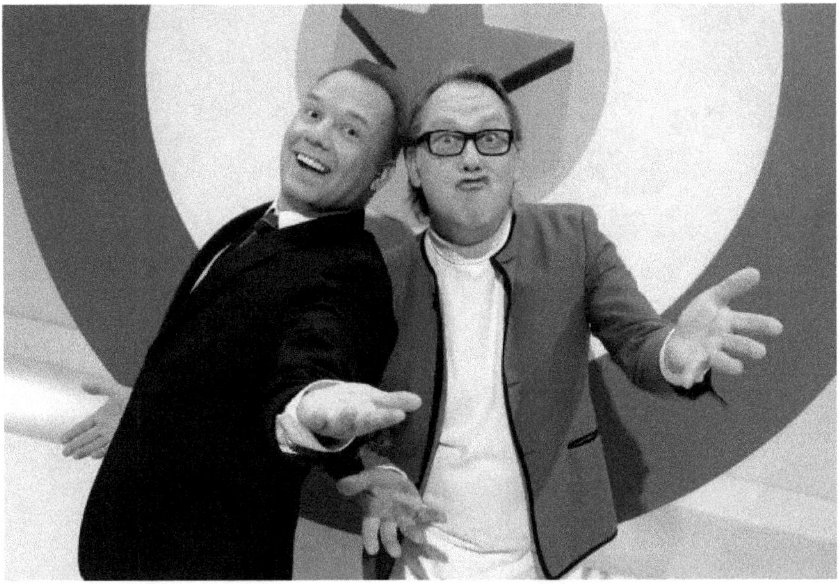

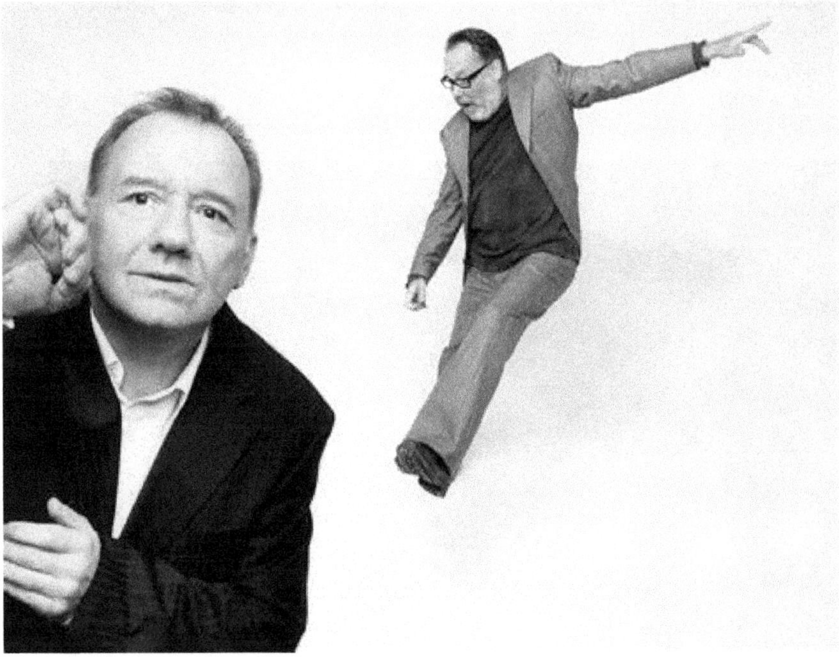

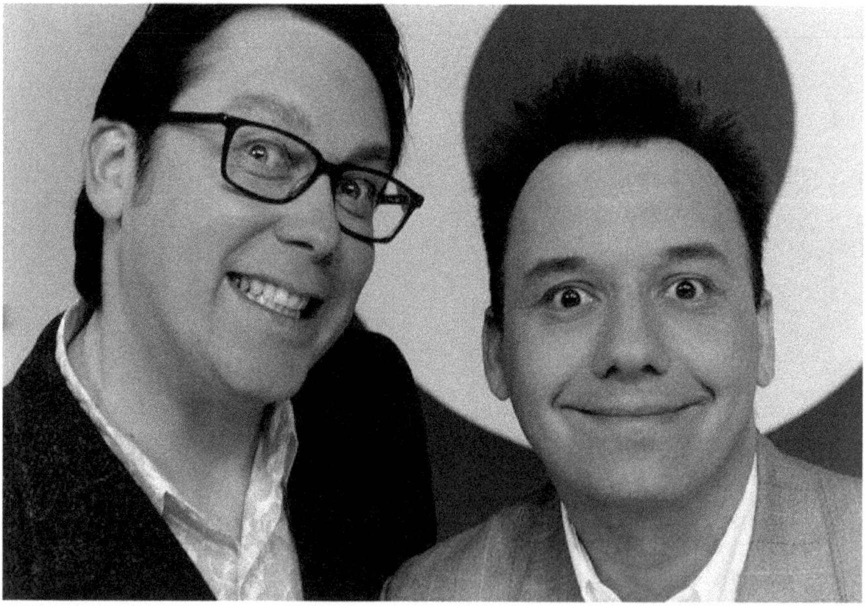

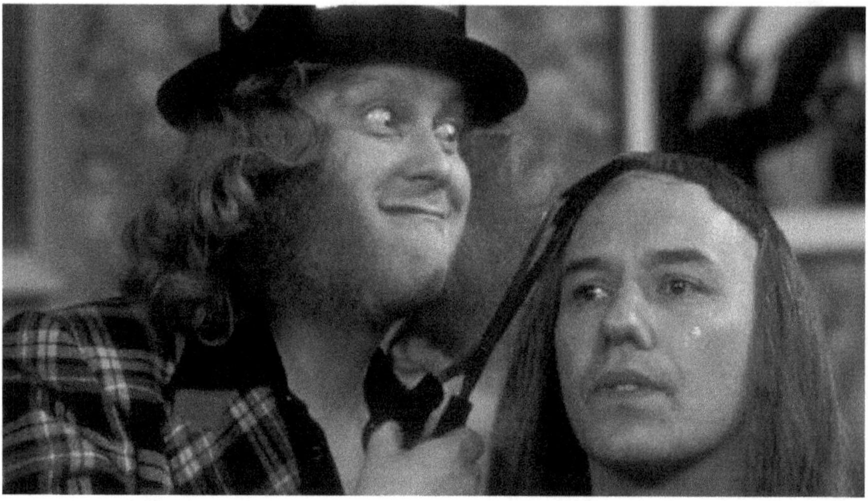

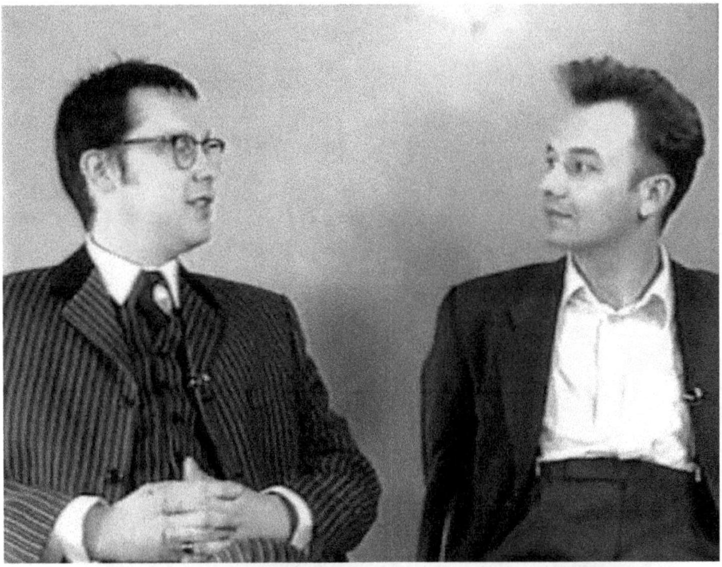

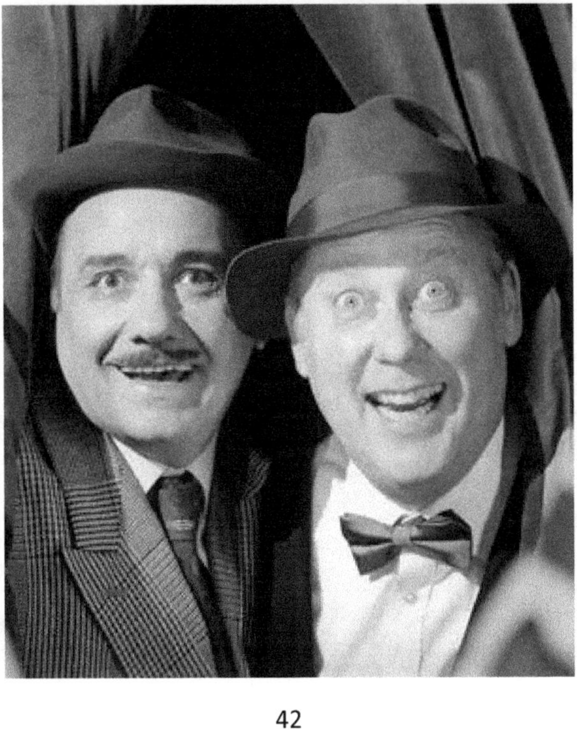

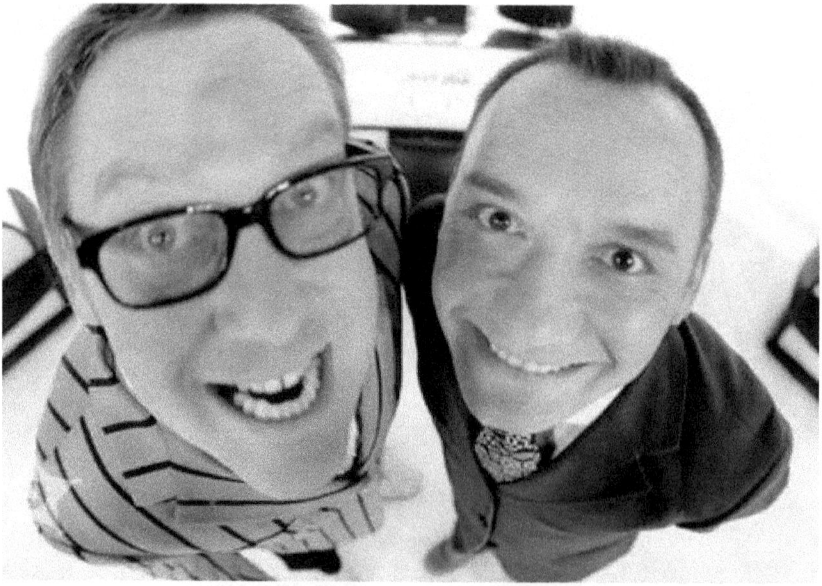

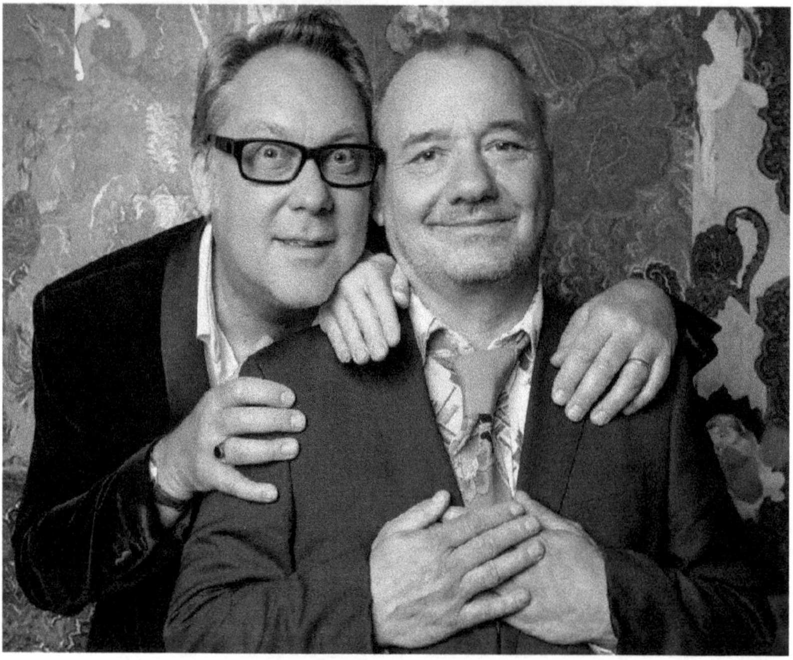

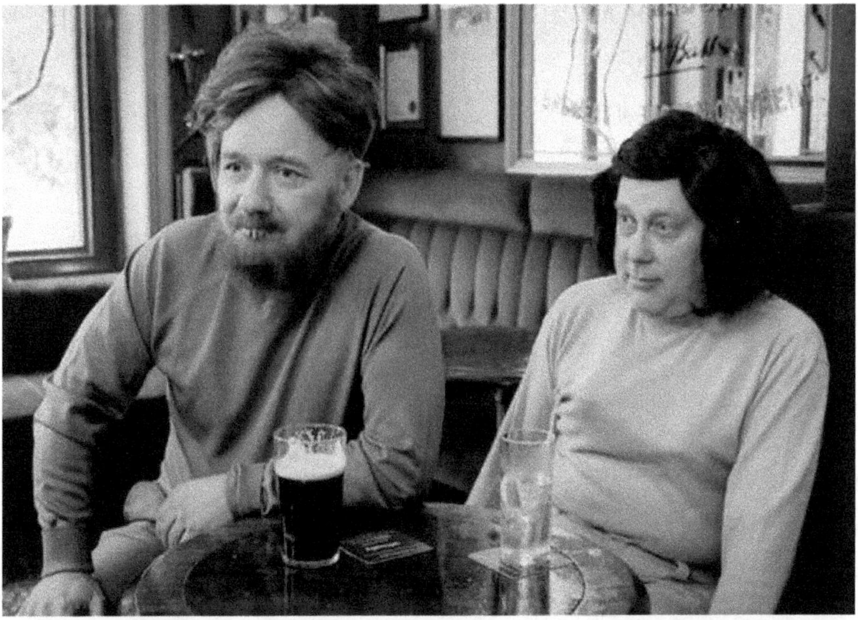

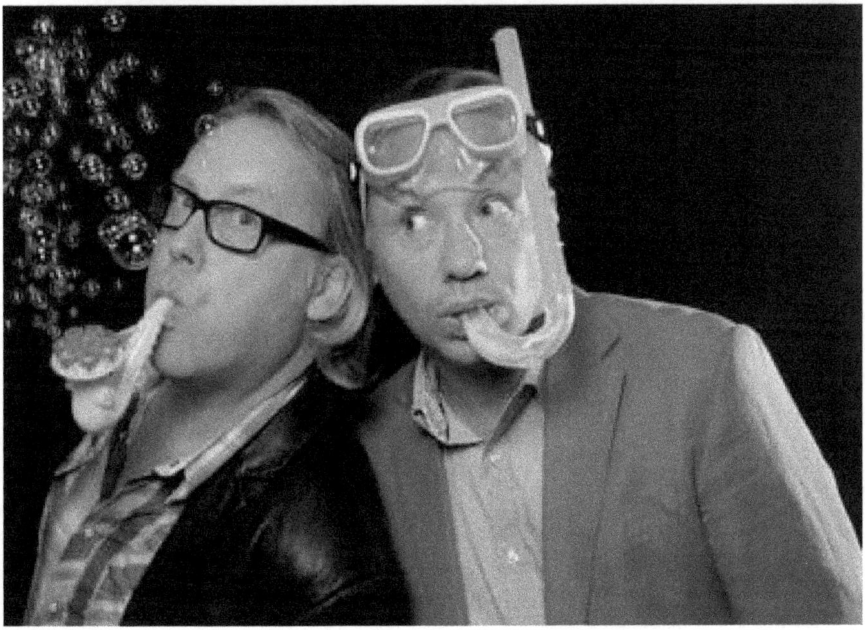

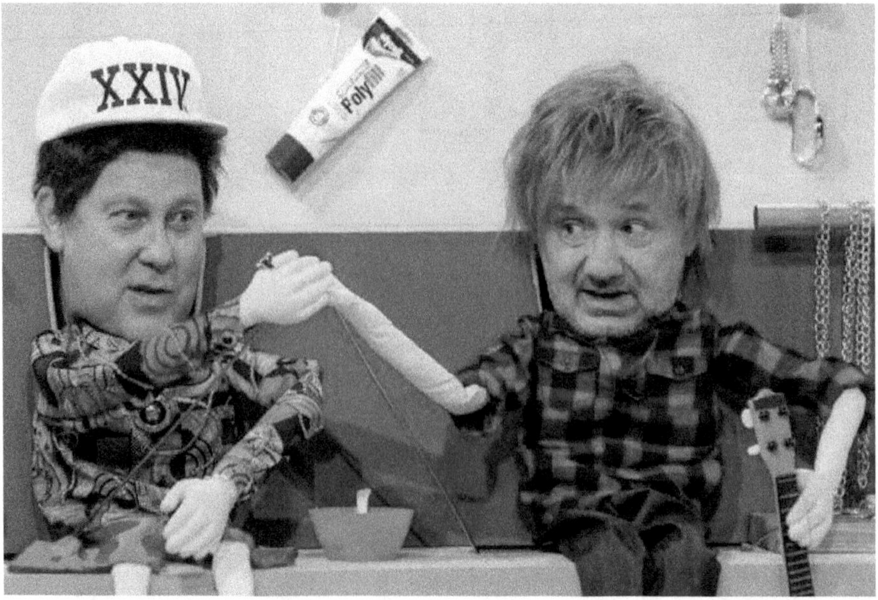
XXIV

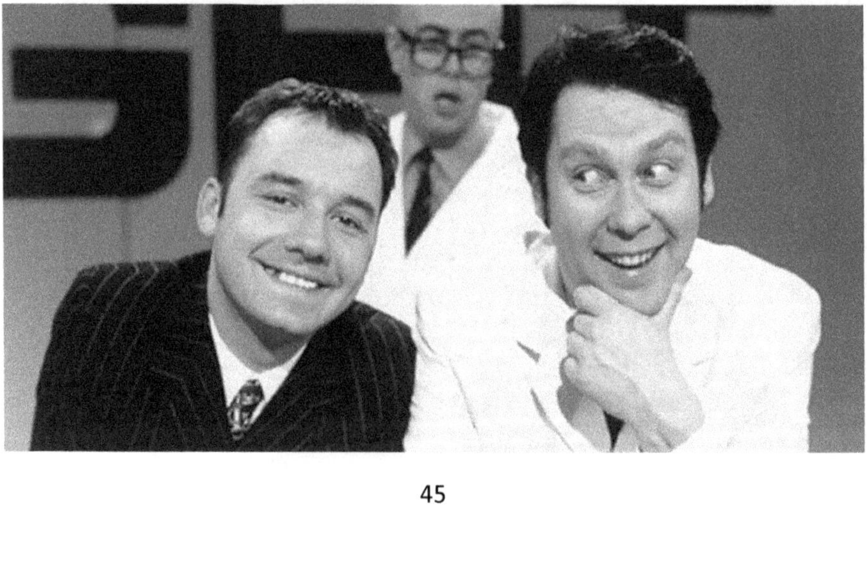

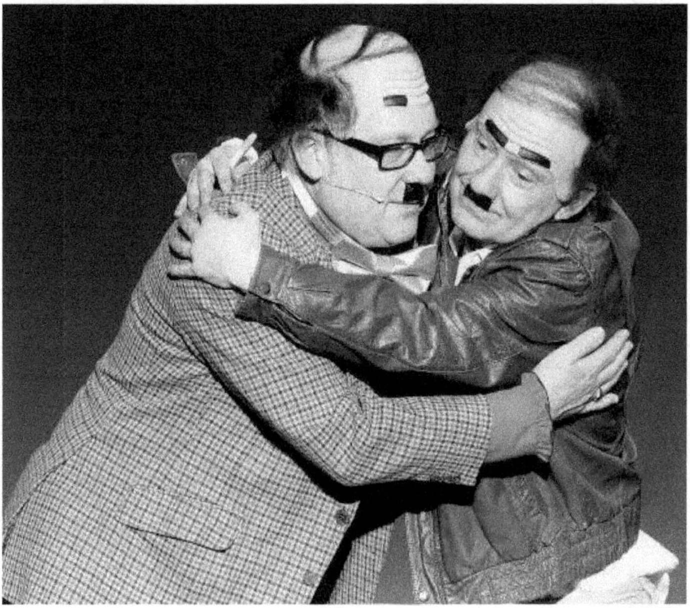

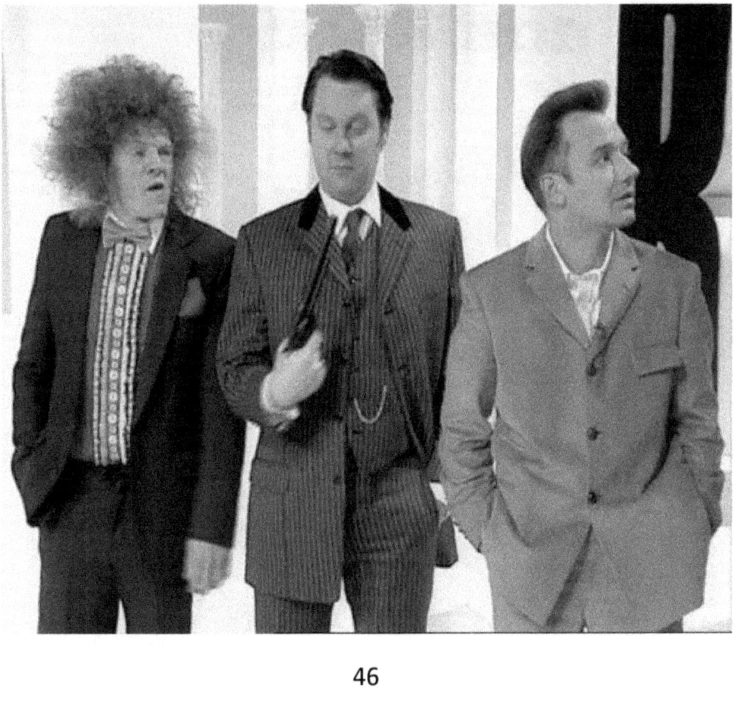

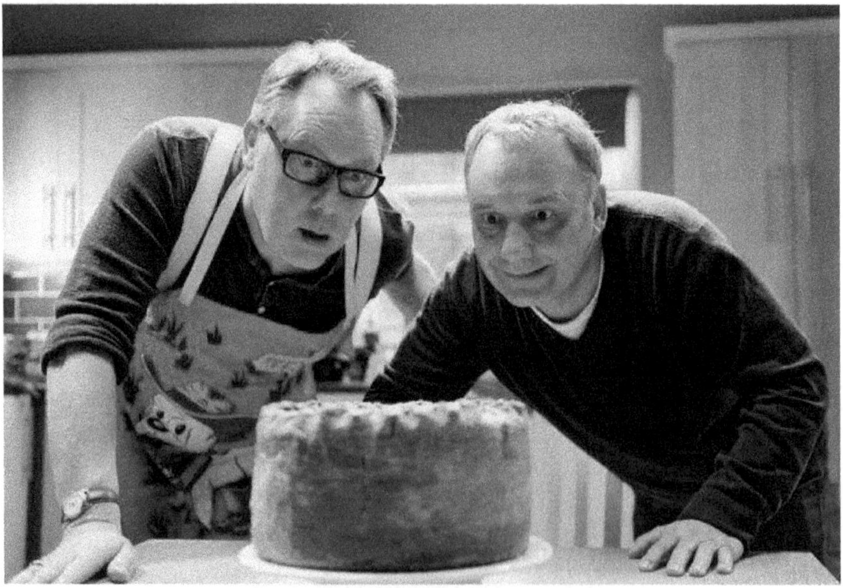

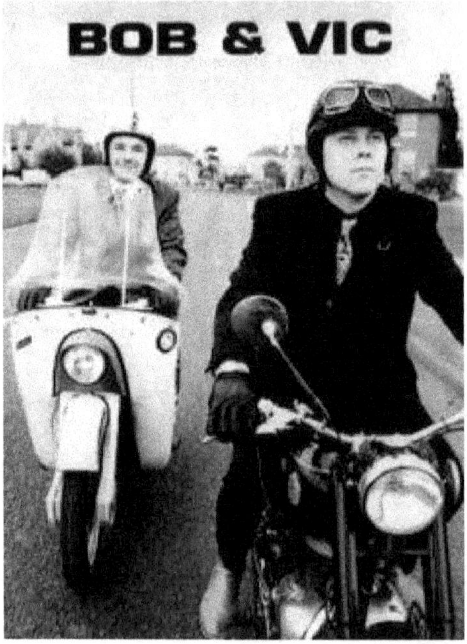
BOB & VIC

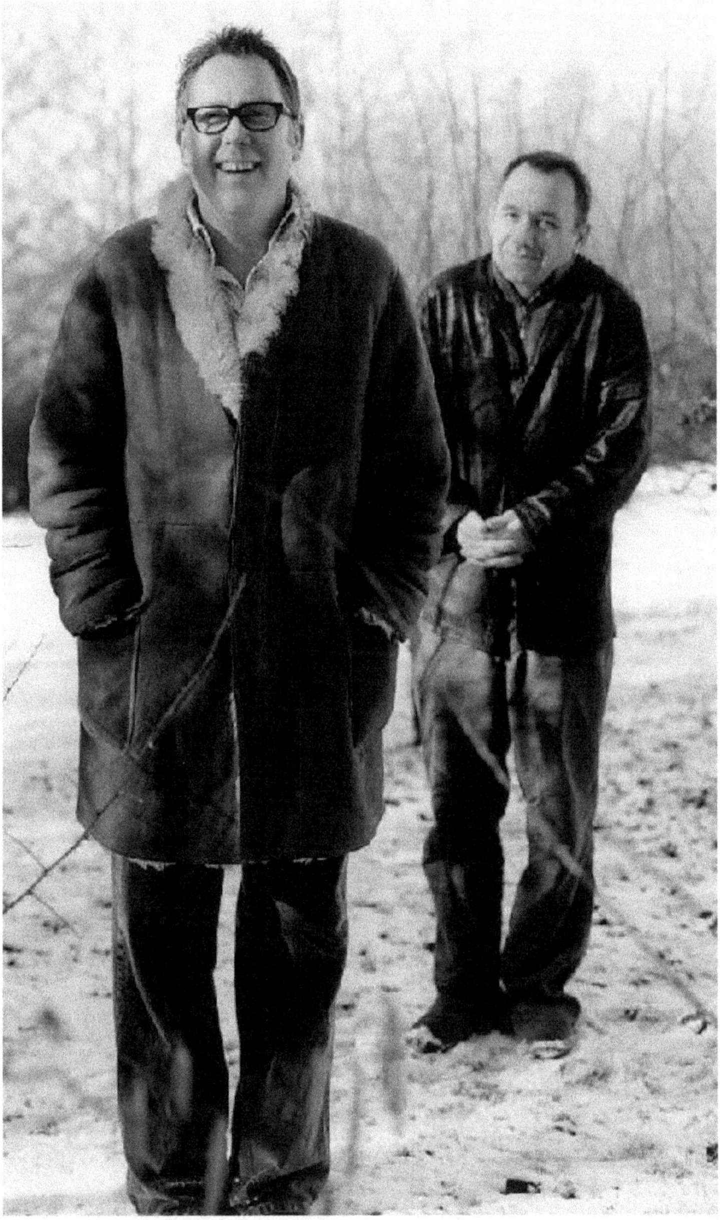

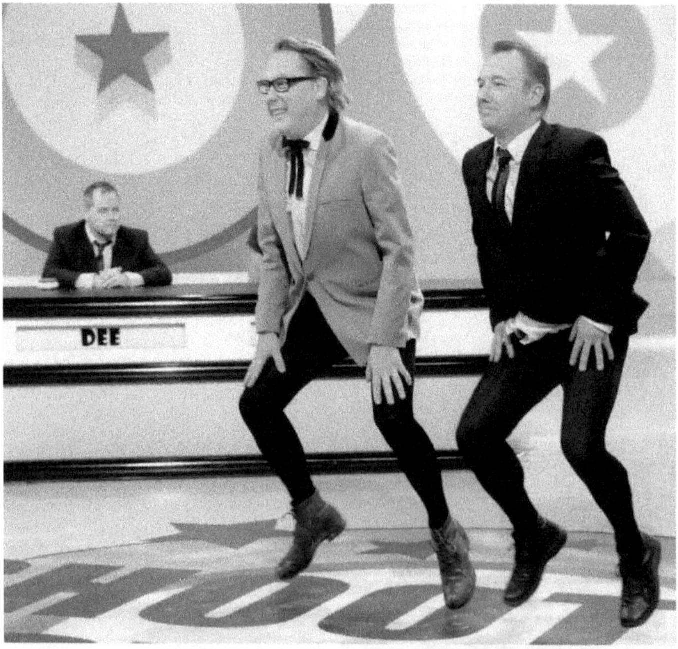
DEE

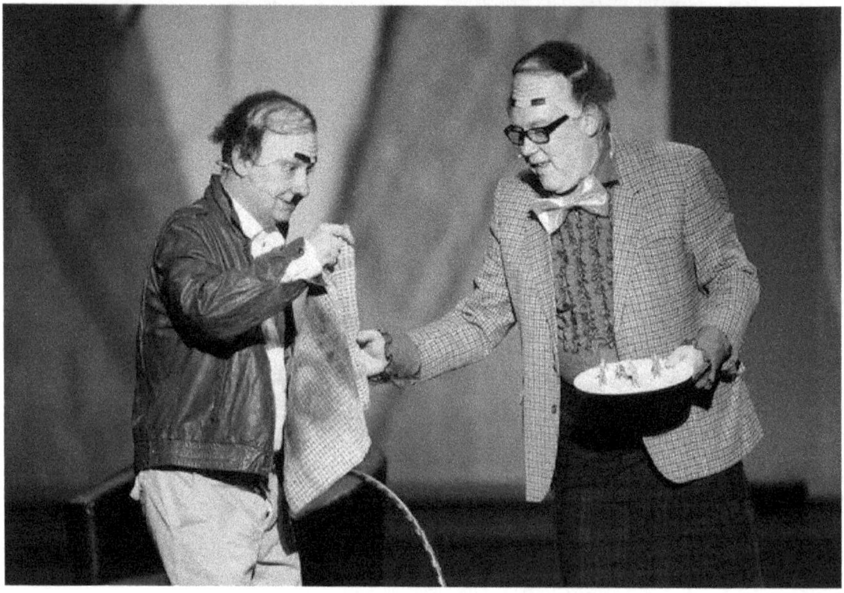

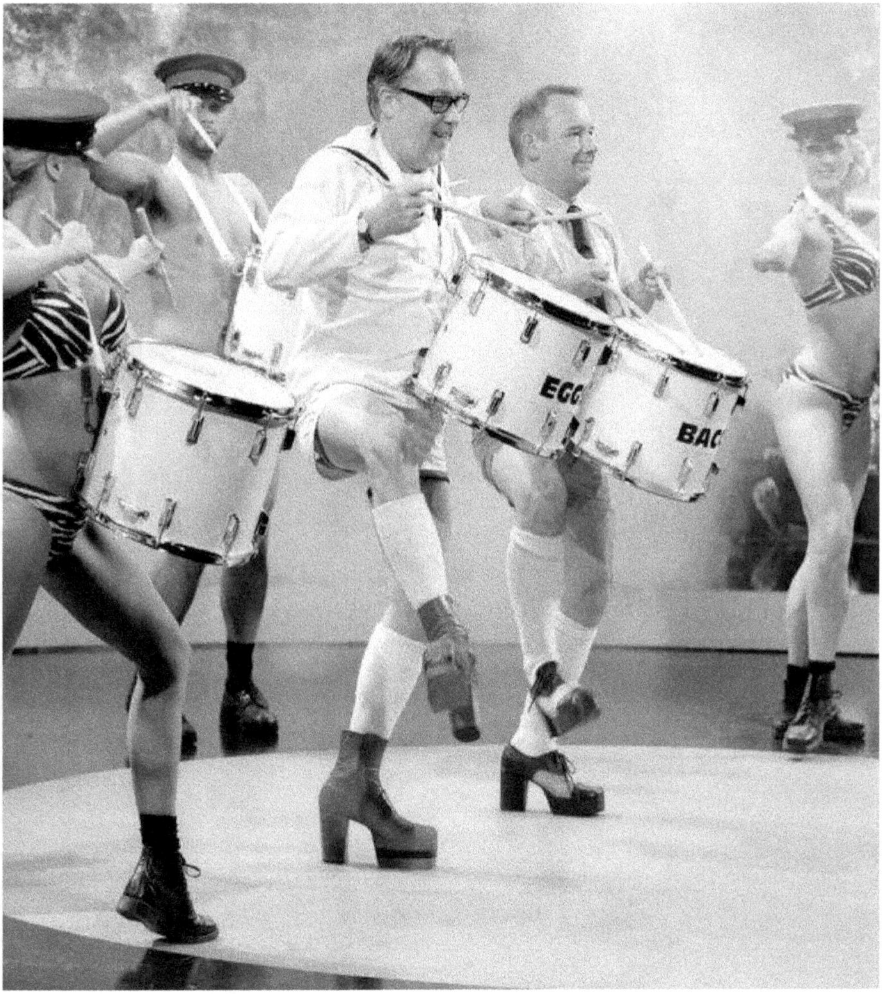

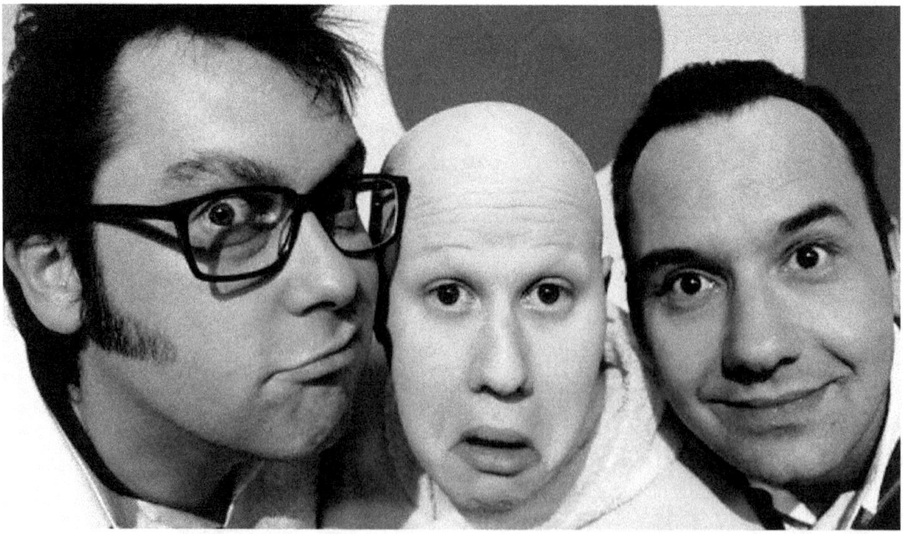

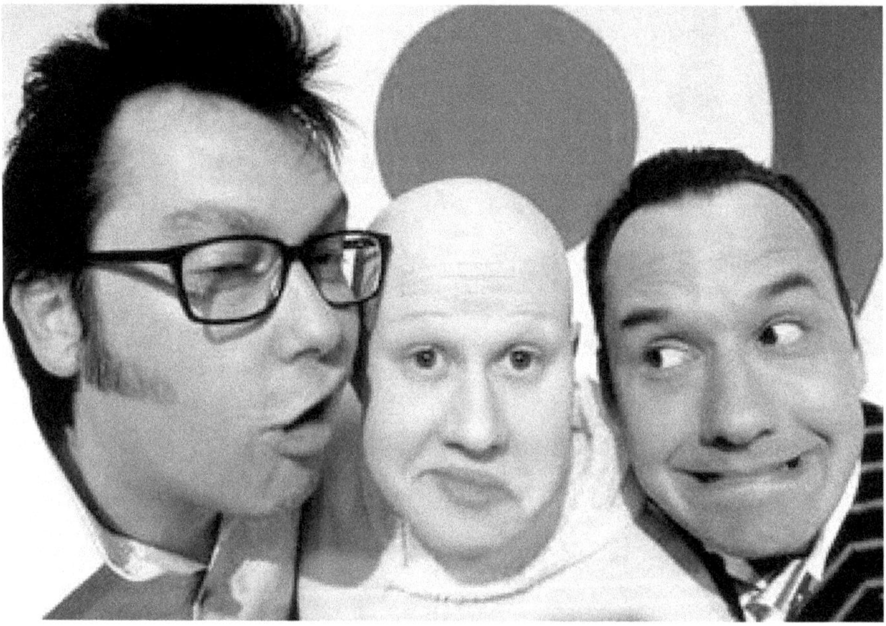

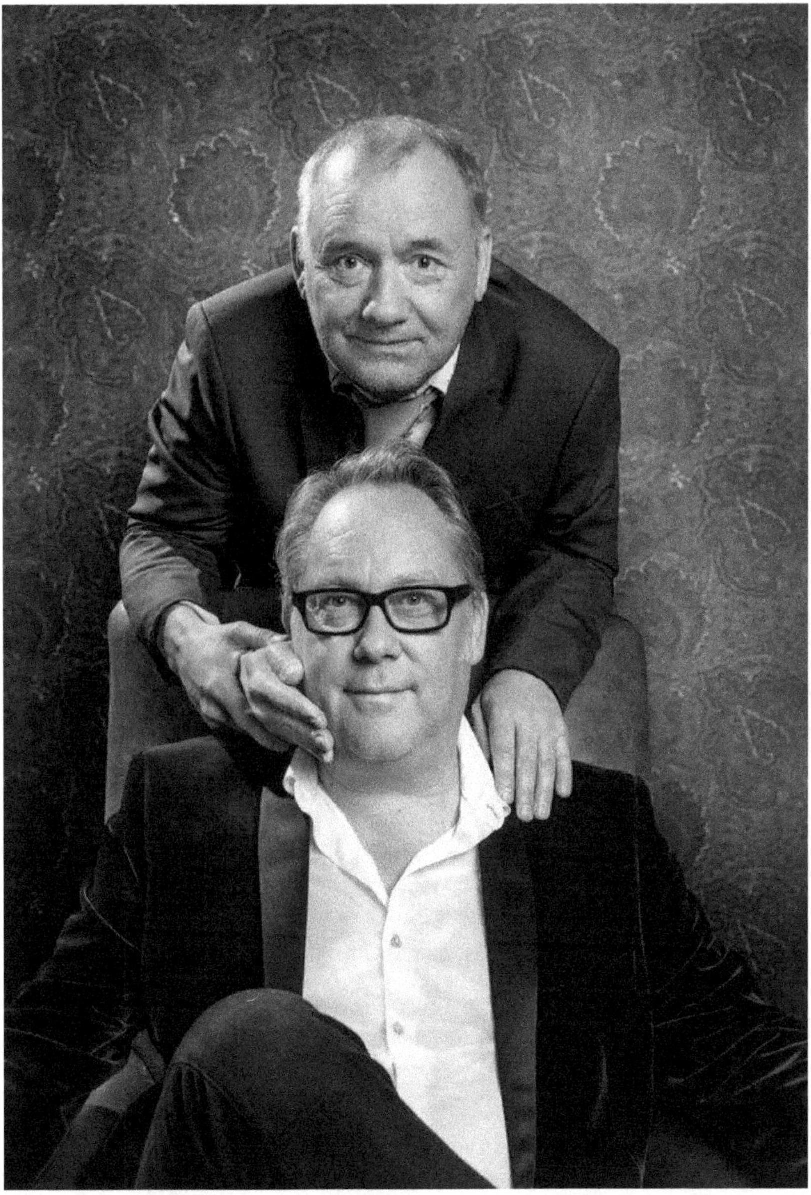

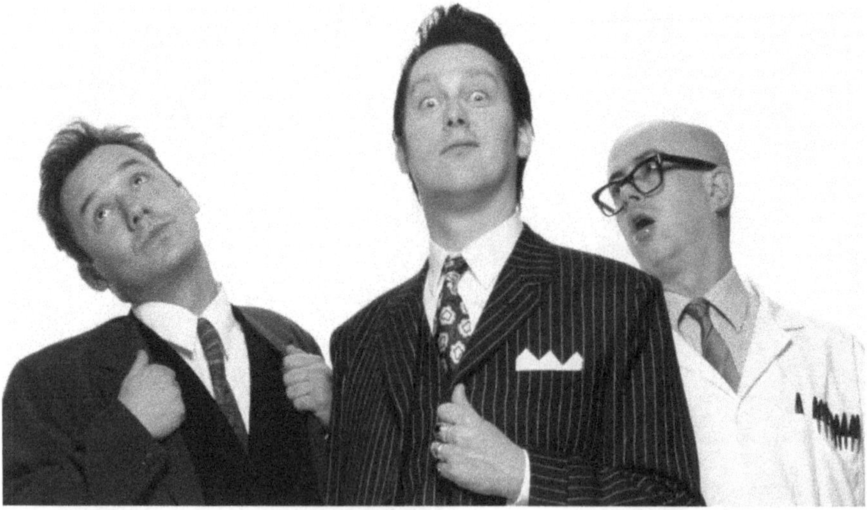

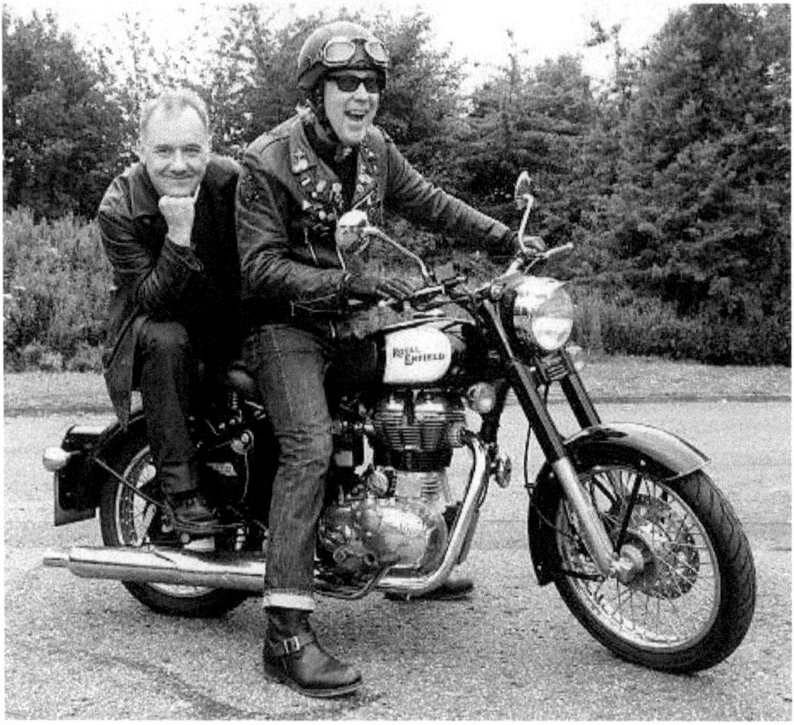
ROYAL ENFIELD

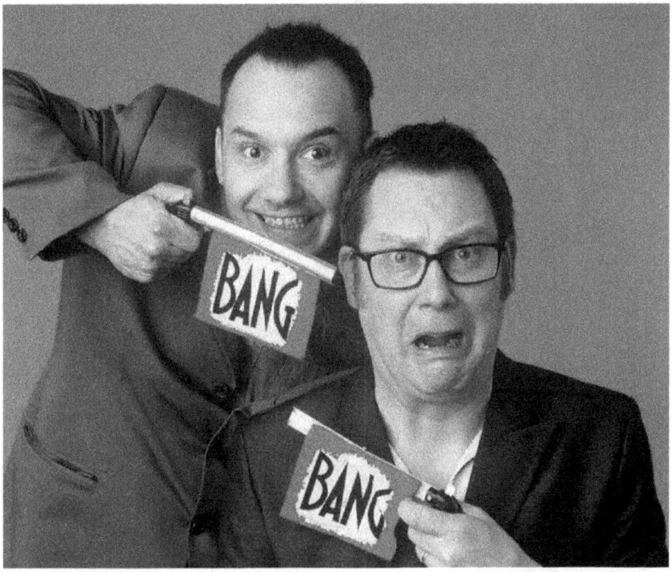
BANG
BANG

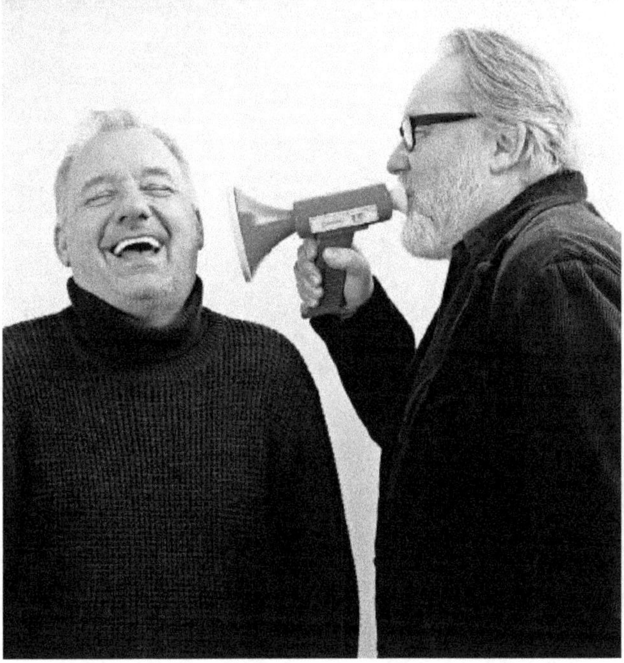

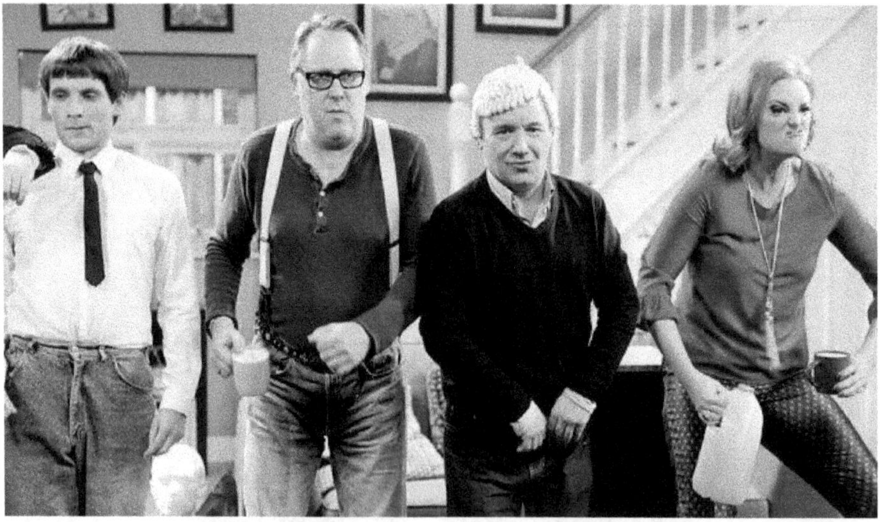

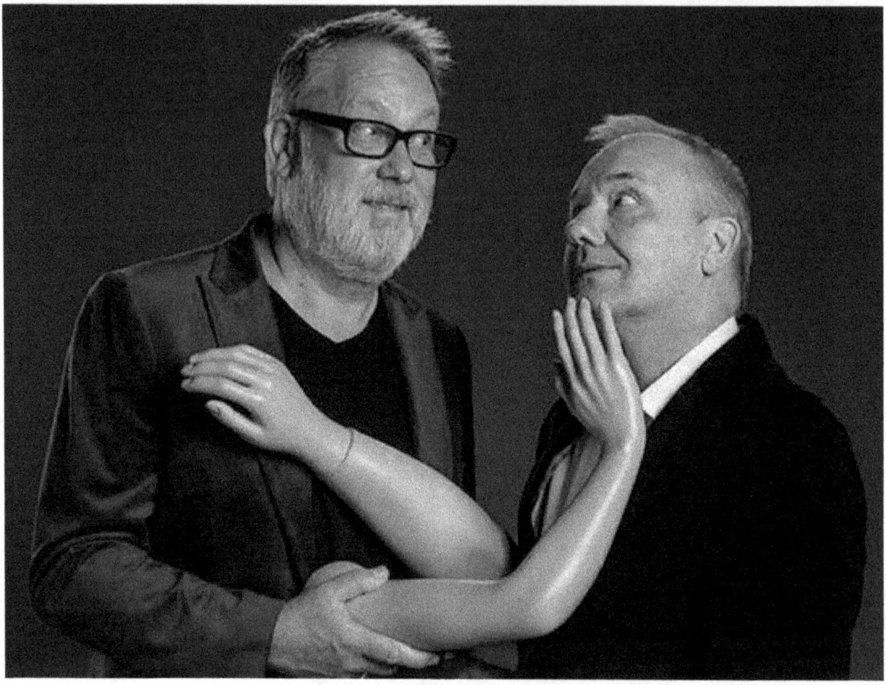

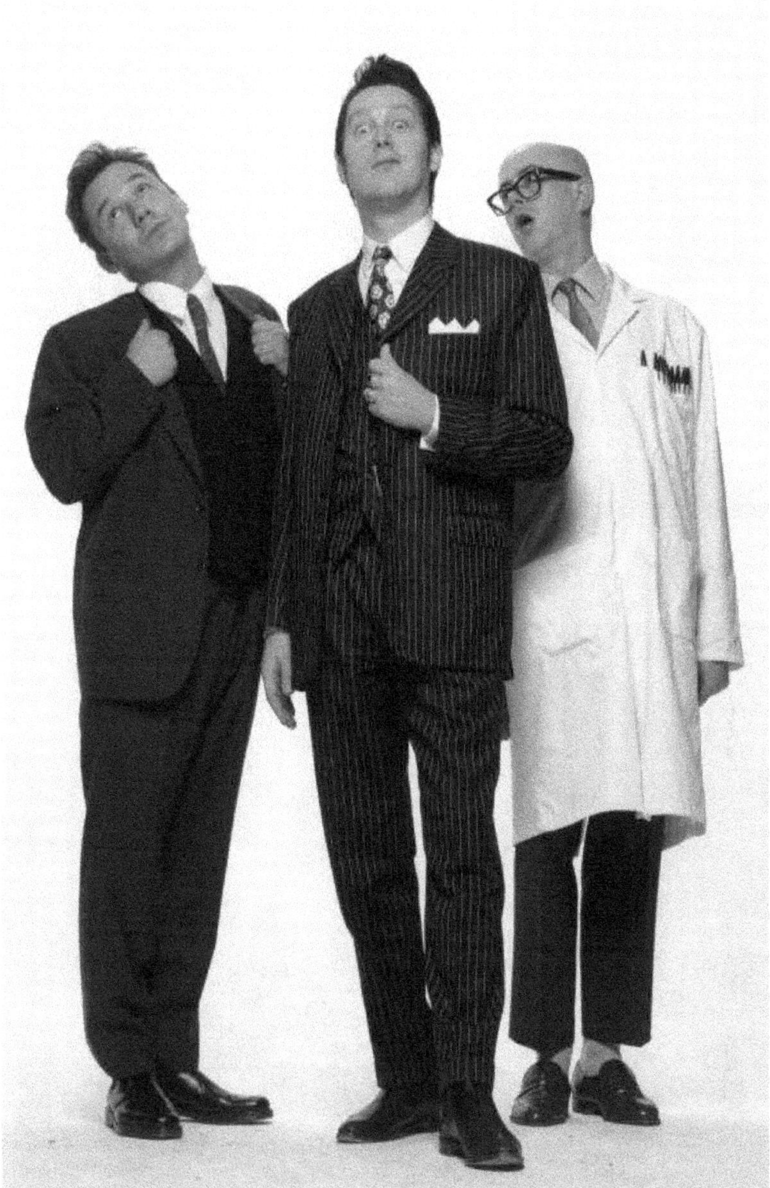

57

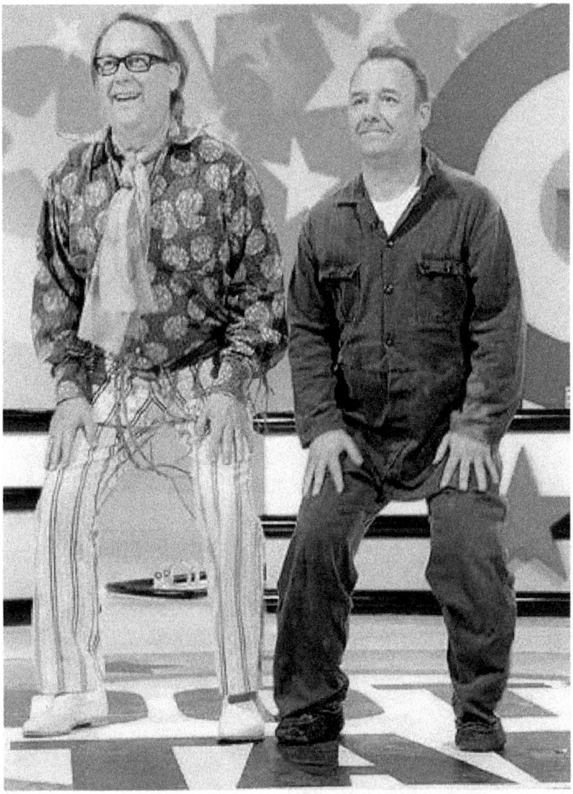

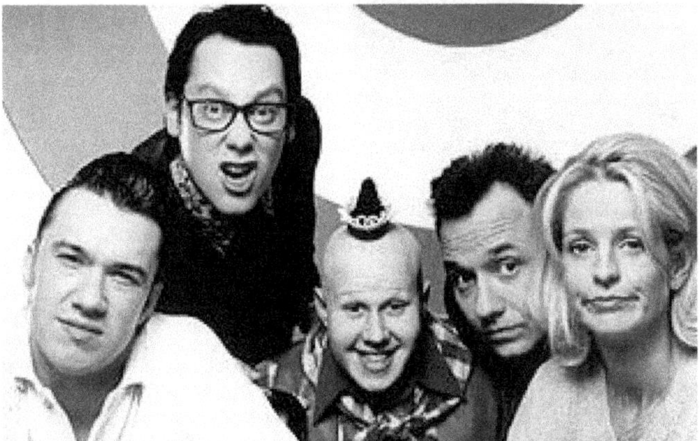

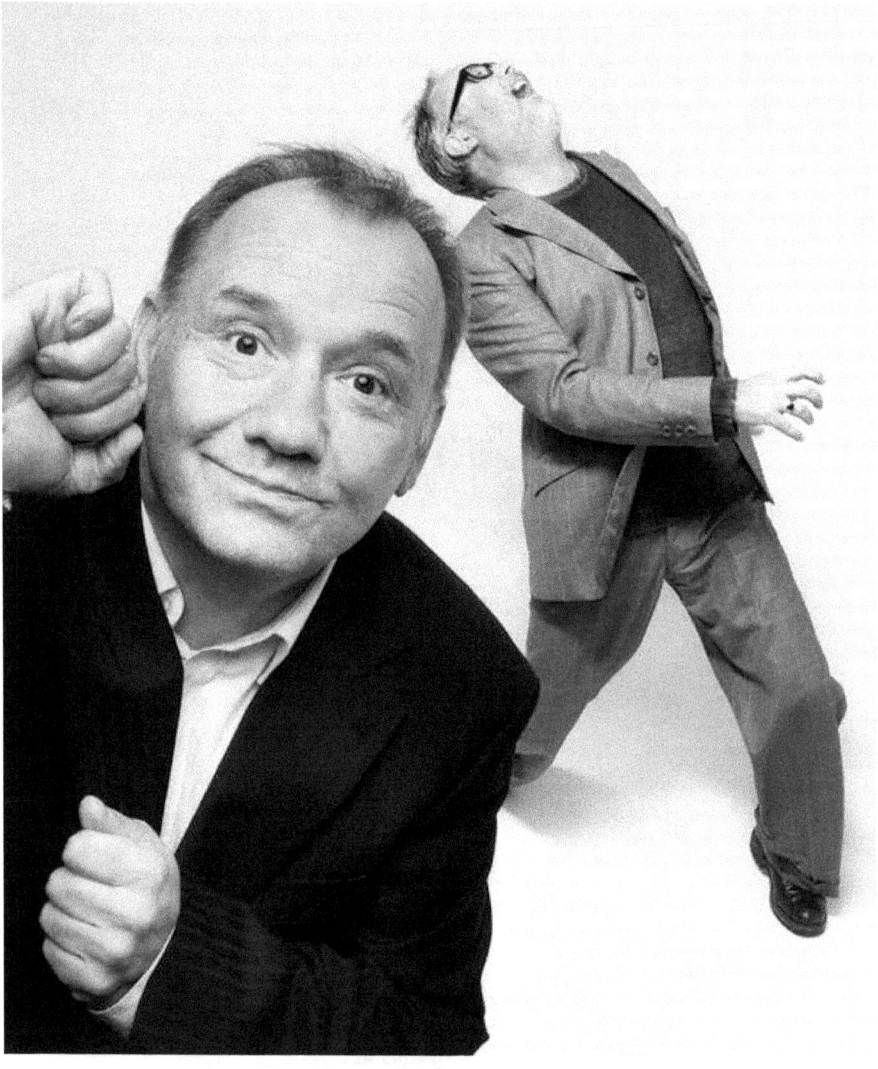

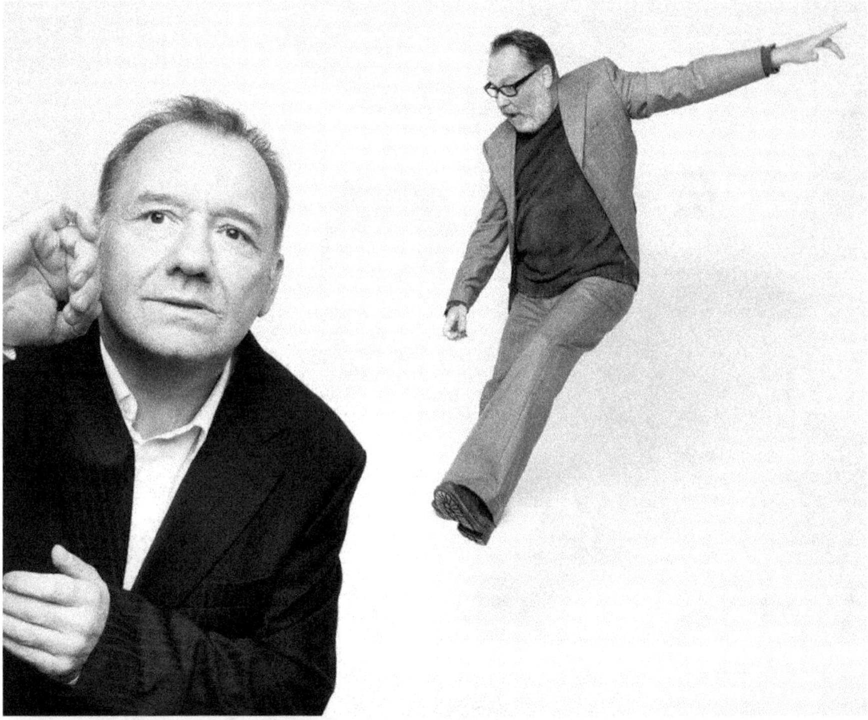

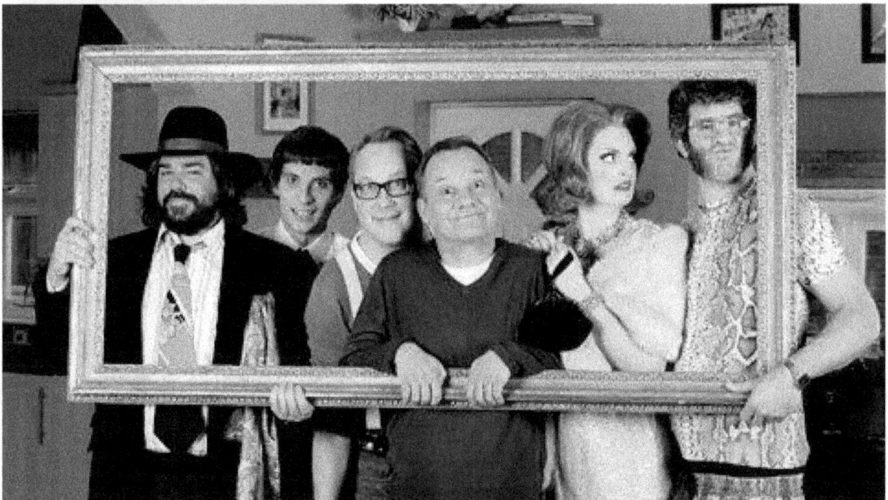

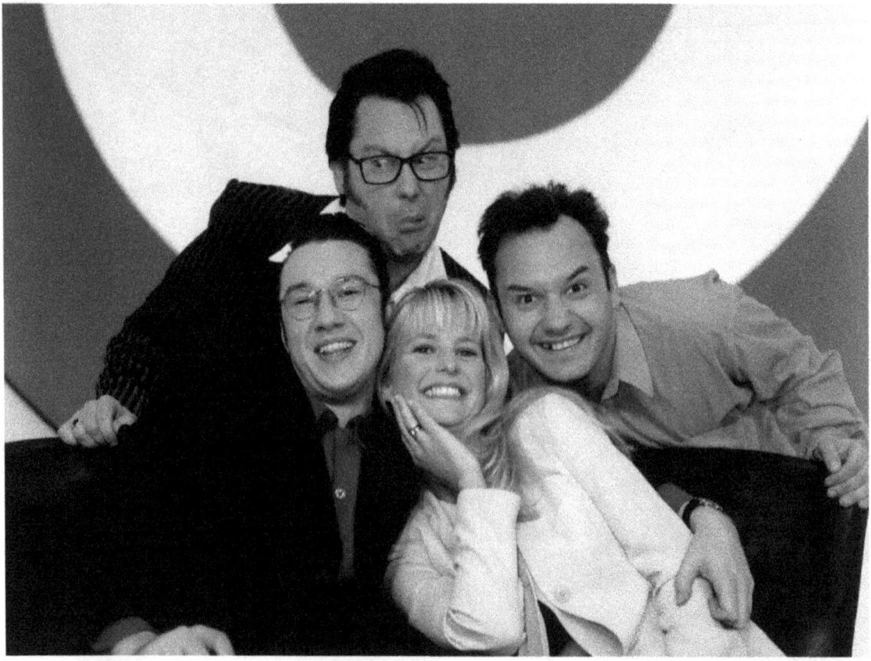

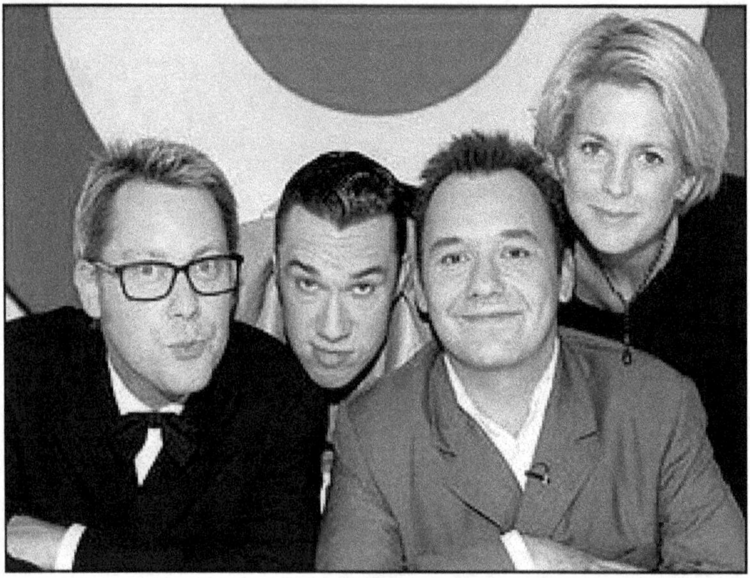

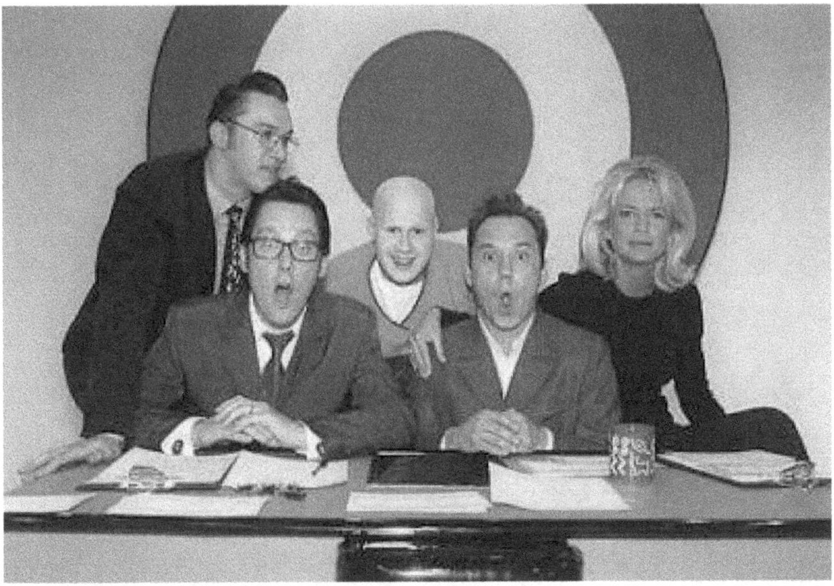

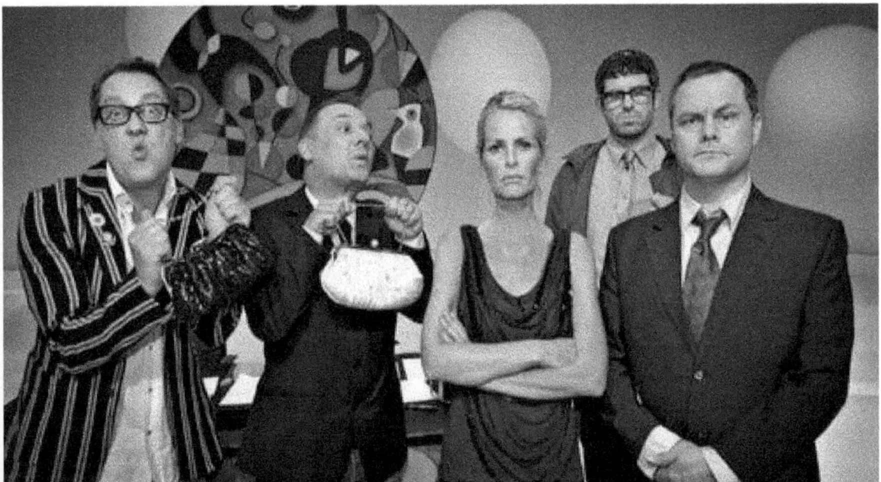

63

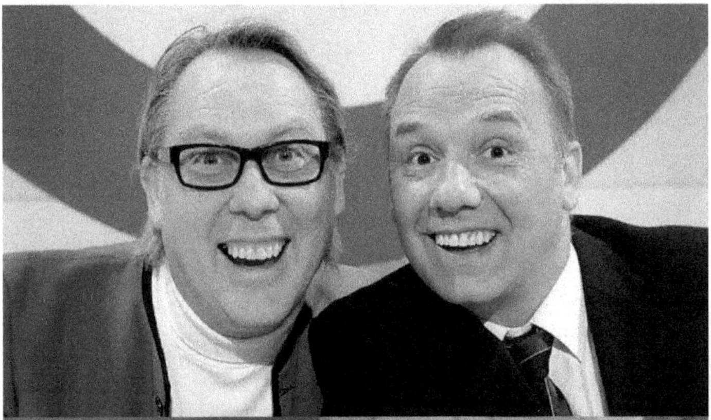

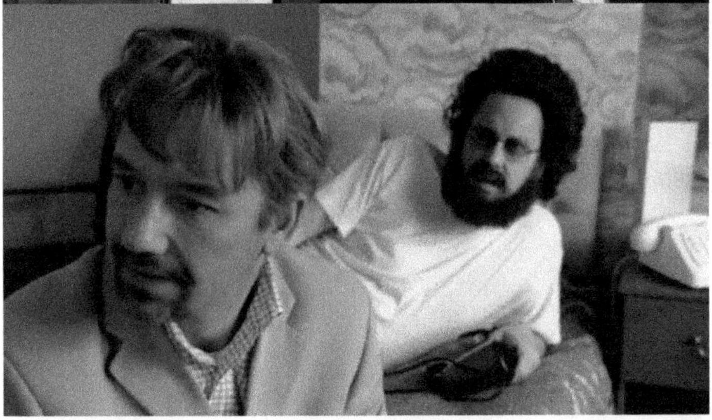

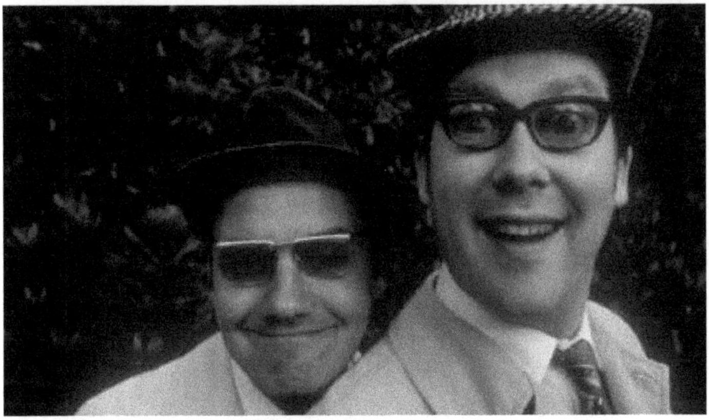

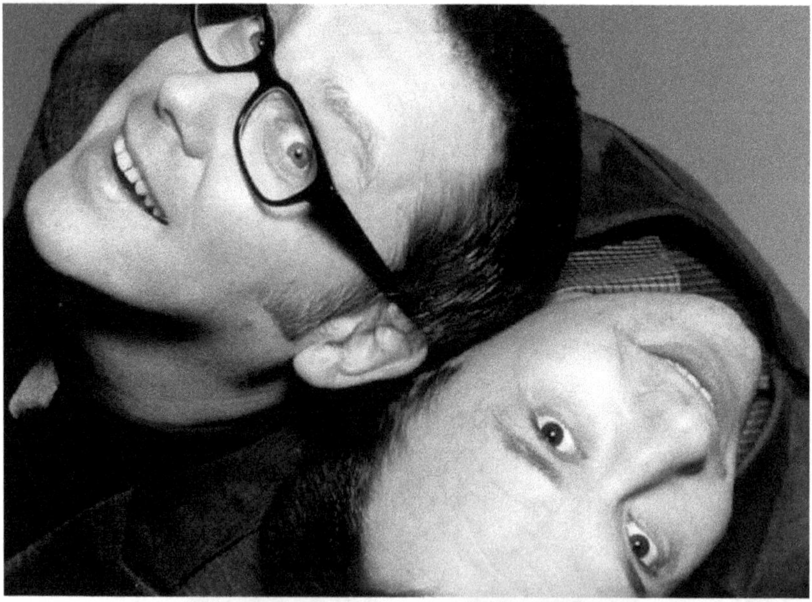

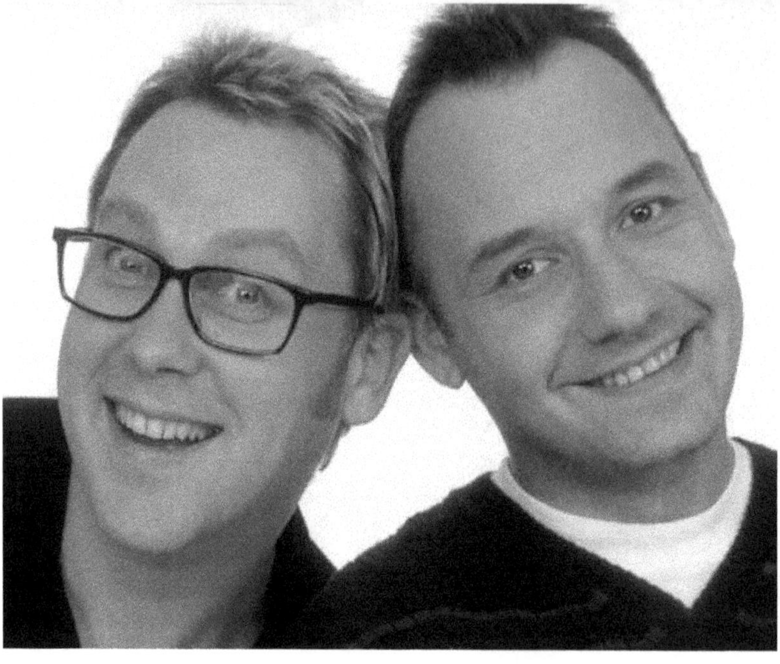

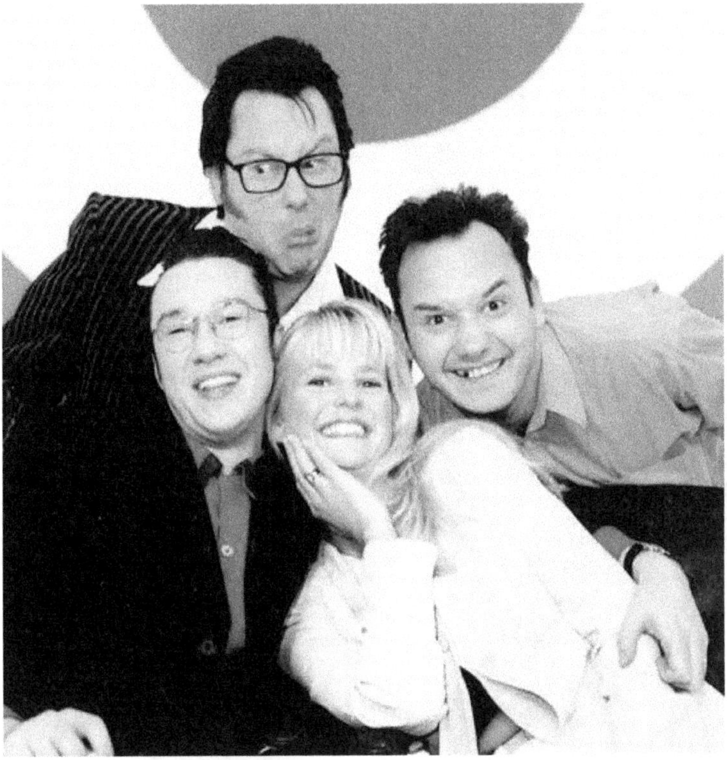

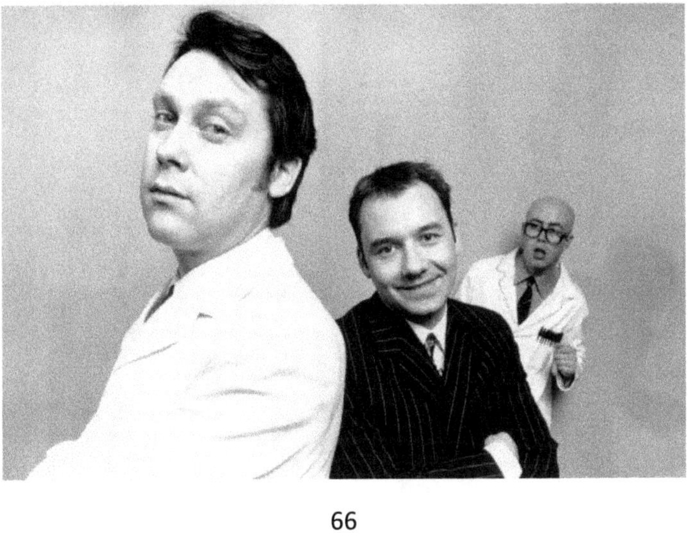

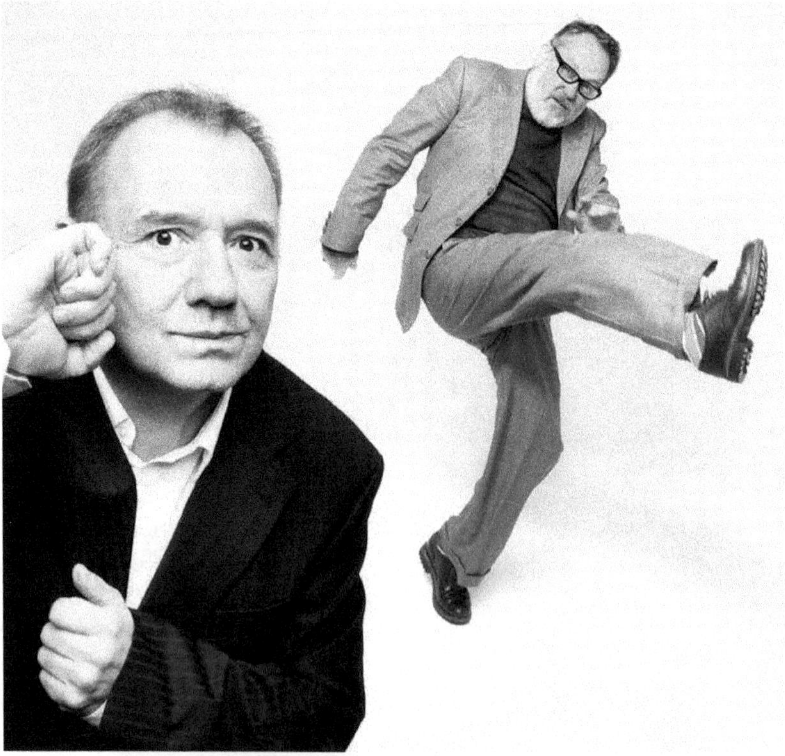

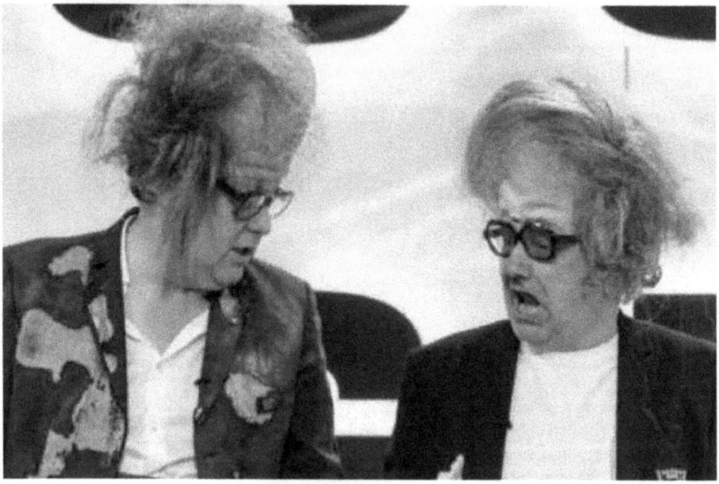

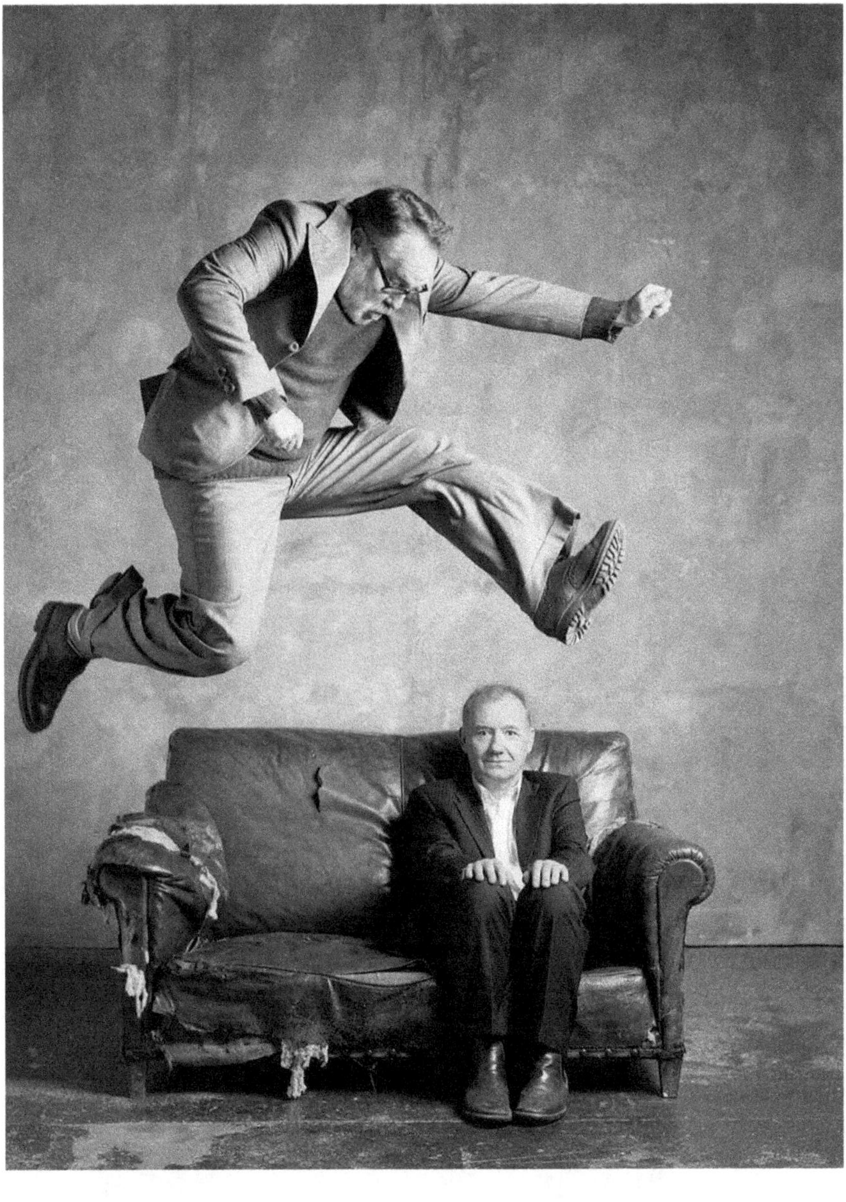

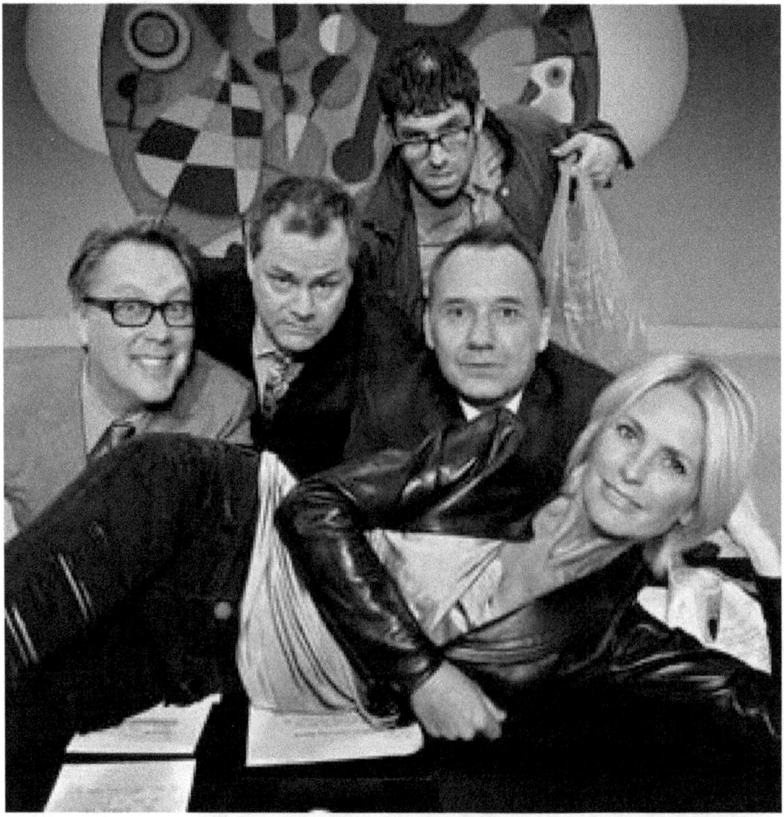

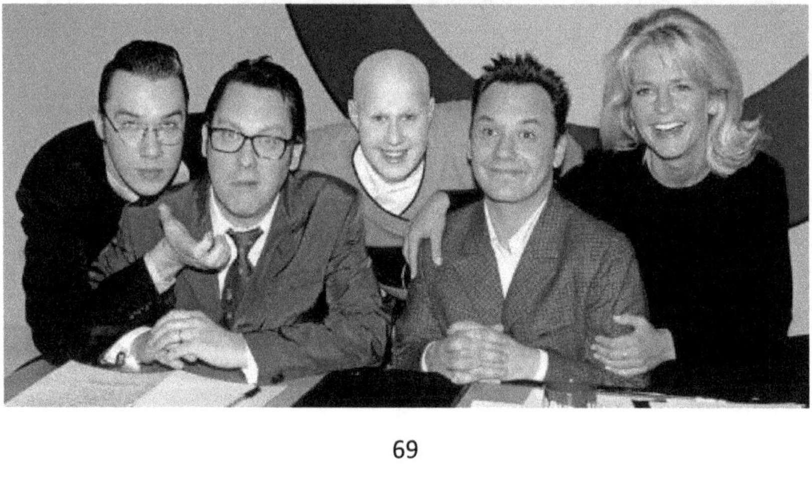

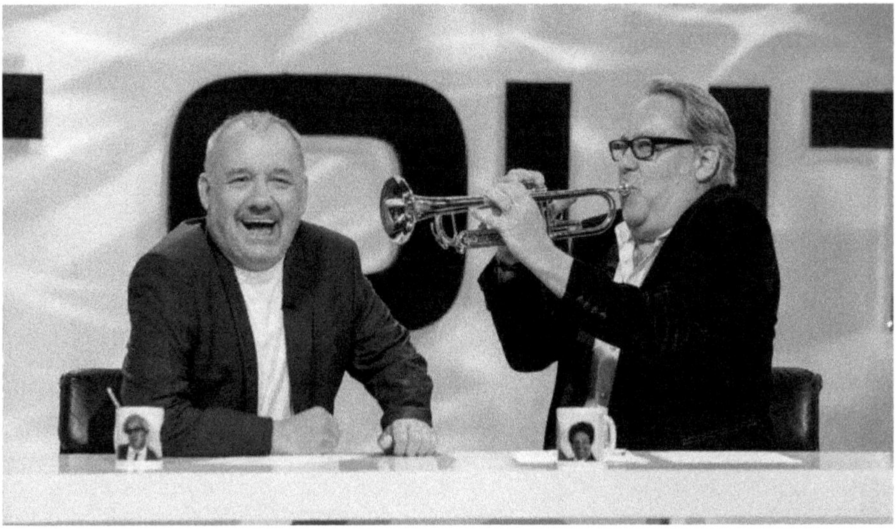

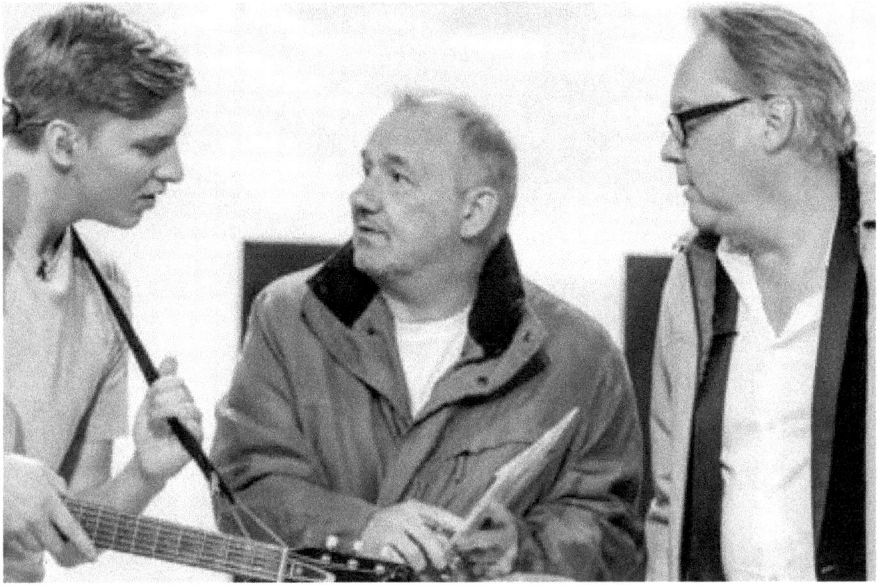

71

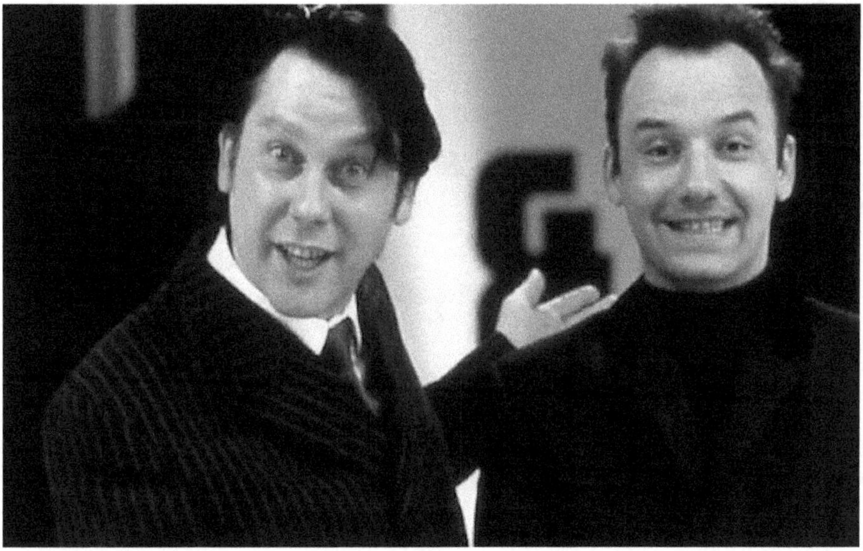

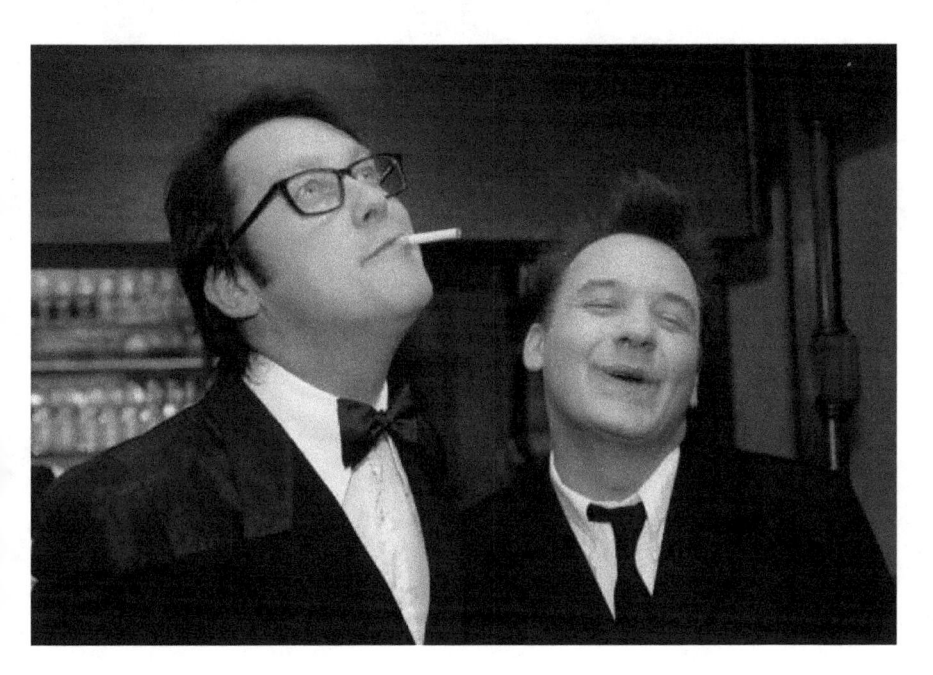

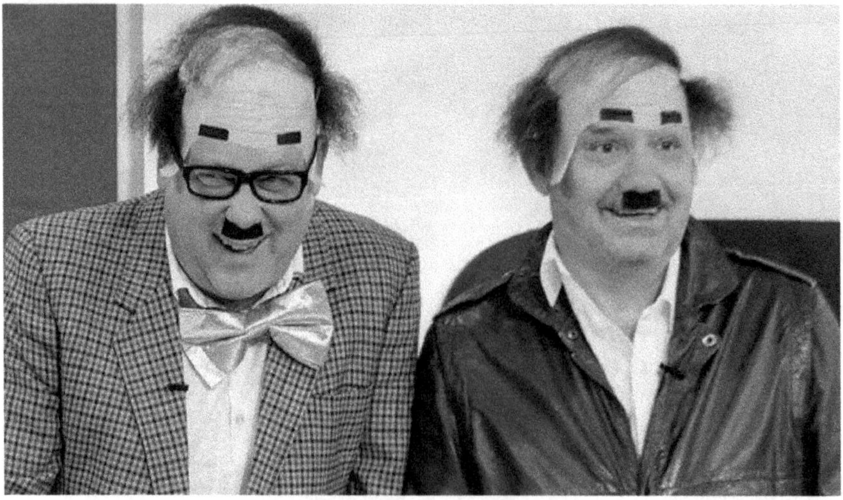

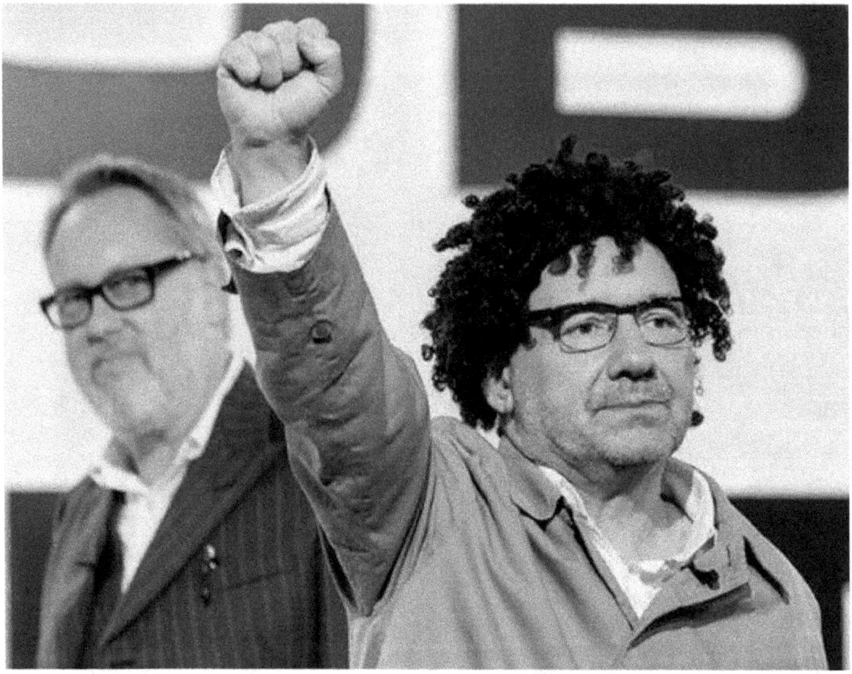

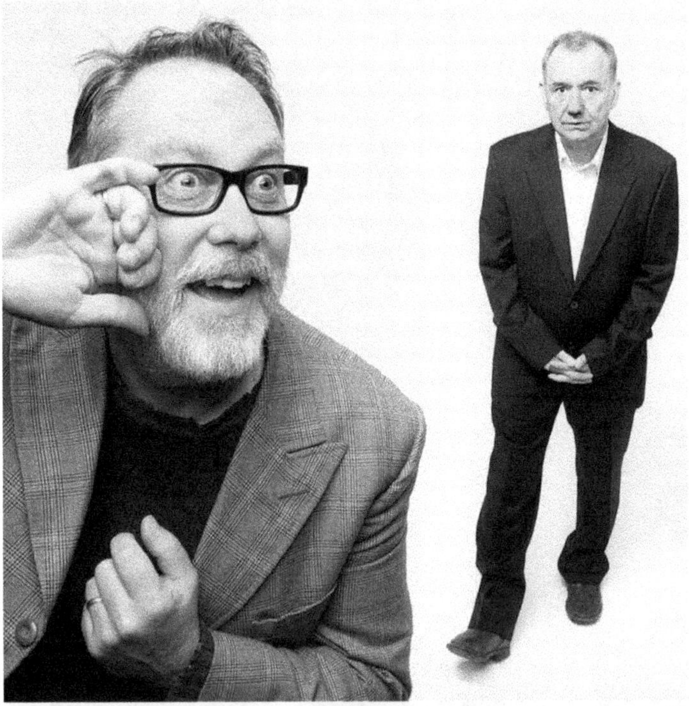

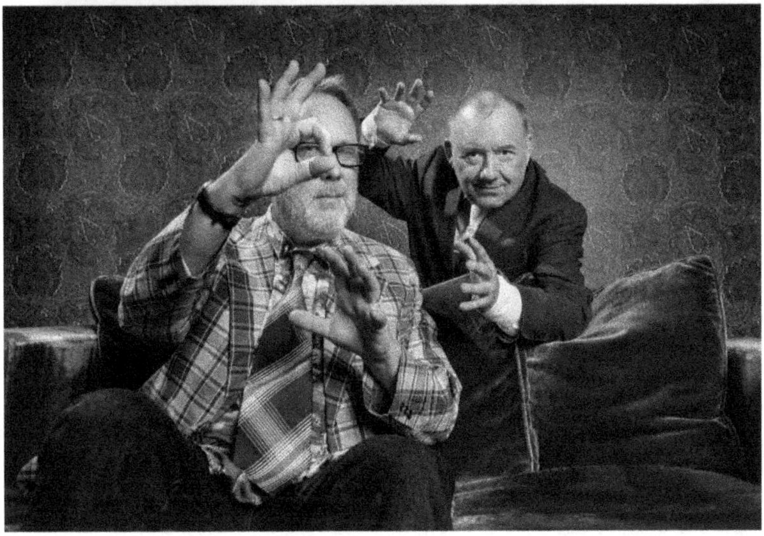

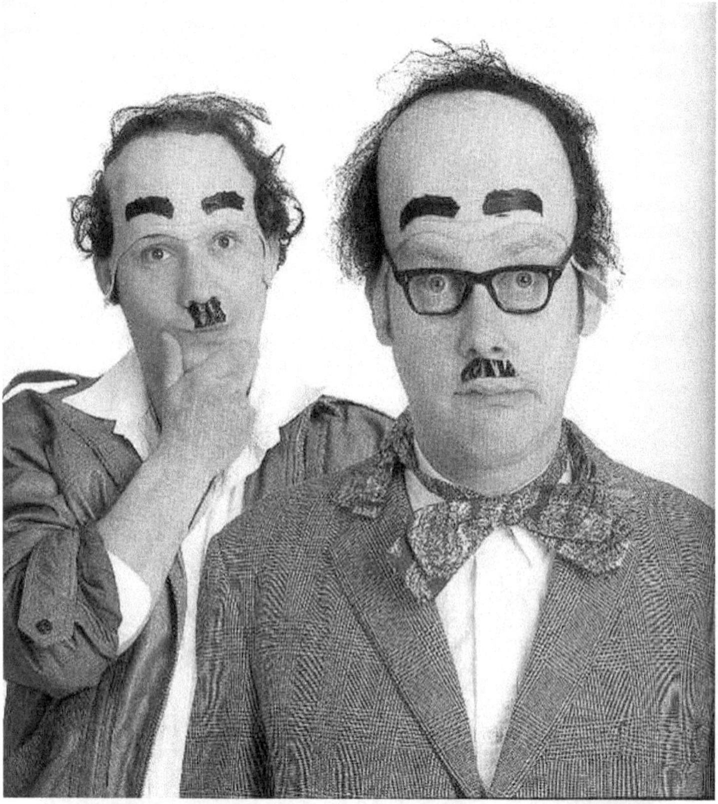

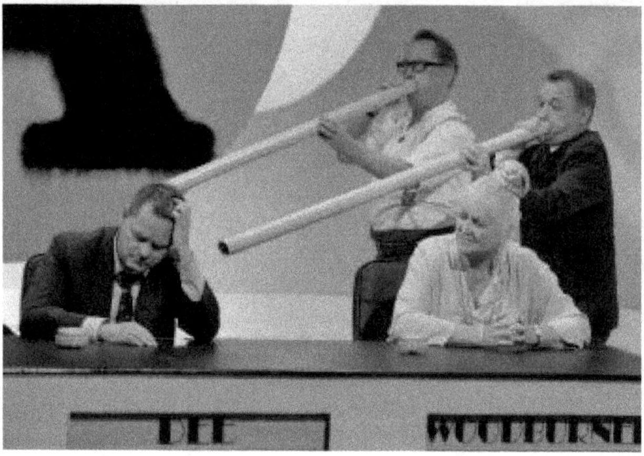

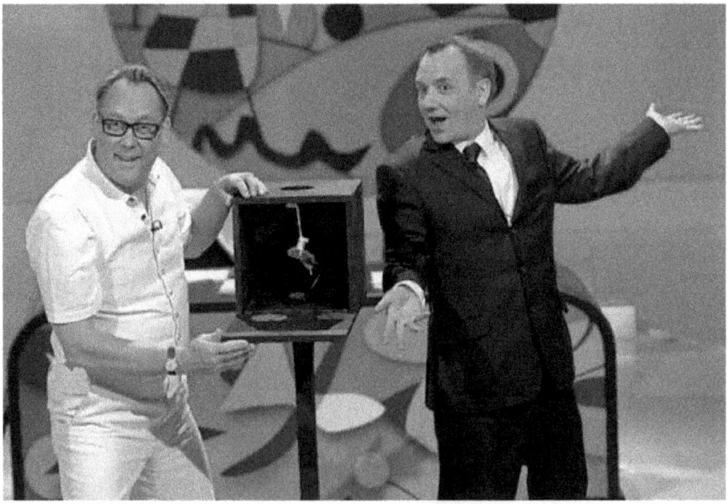

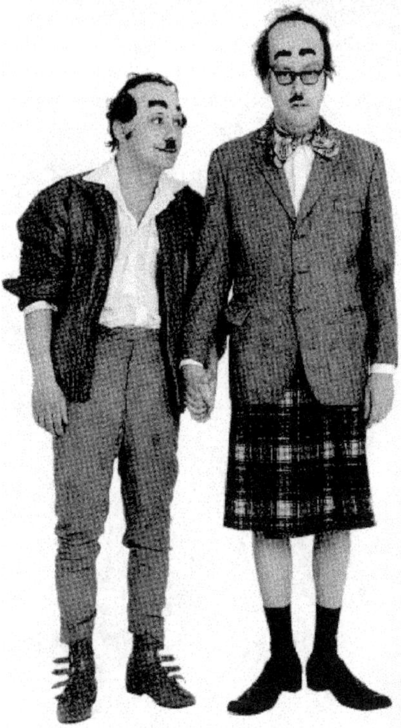

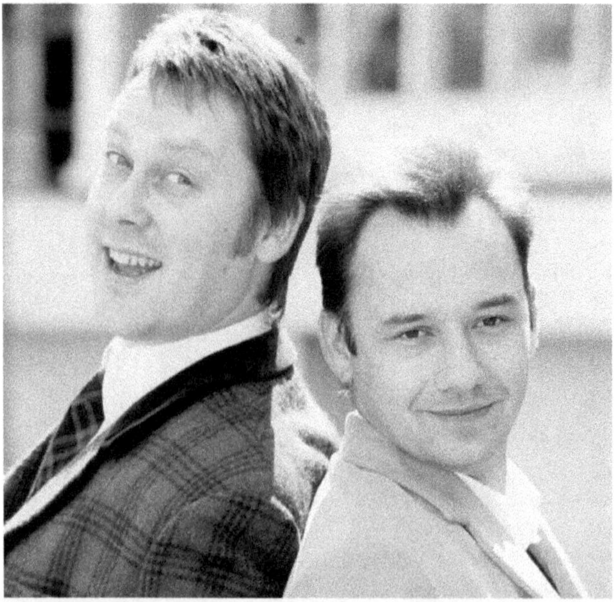

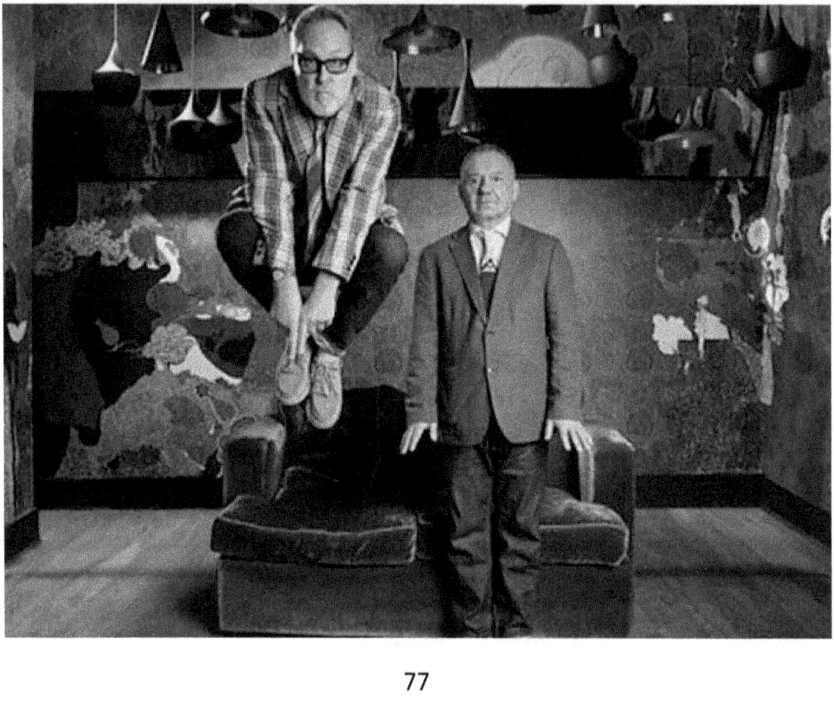

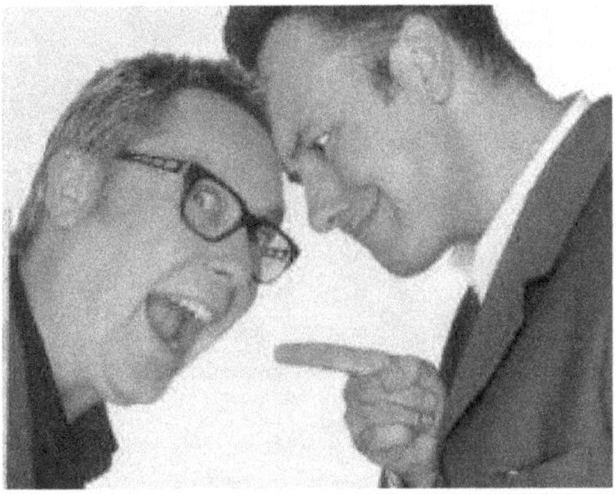

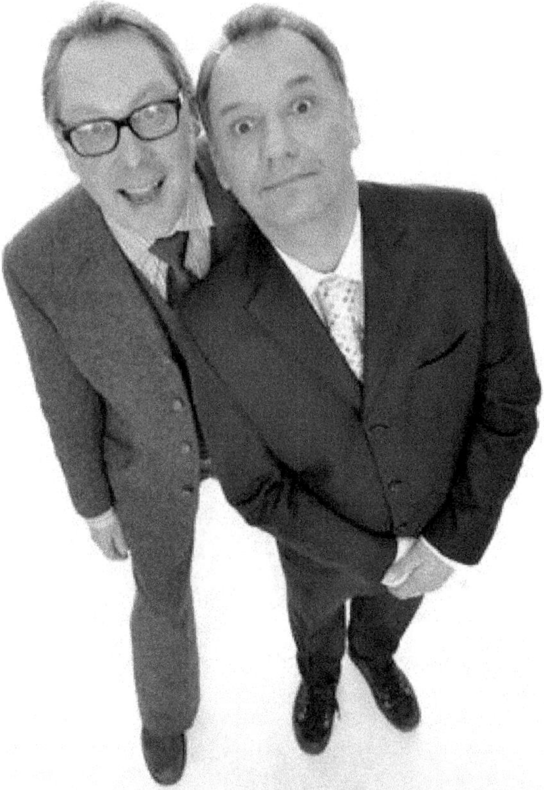

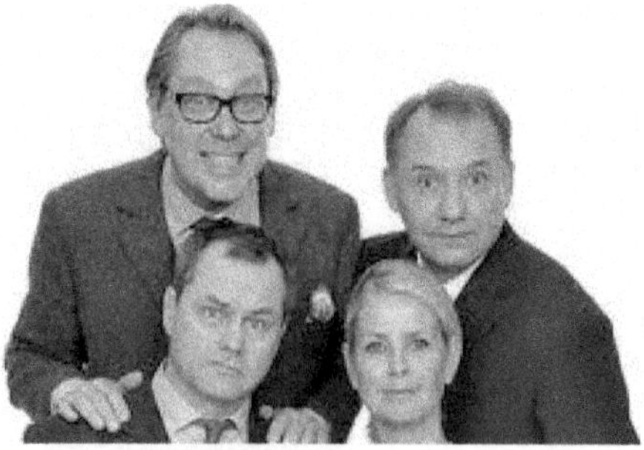

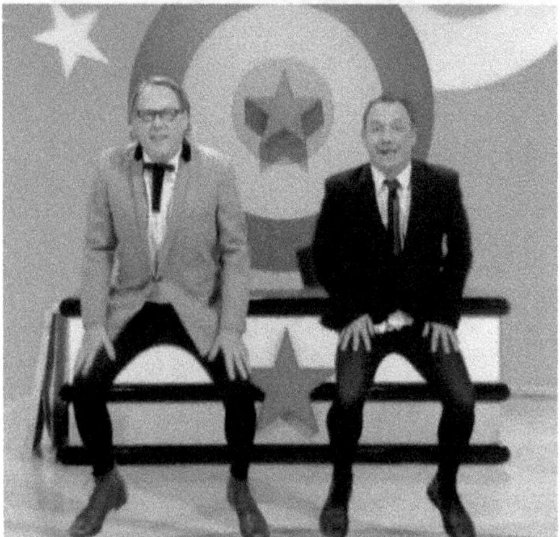

80

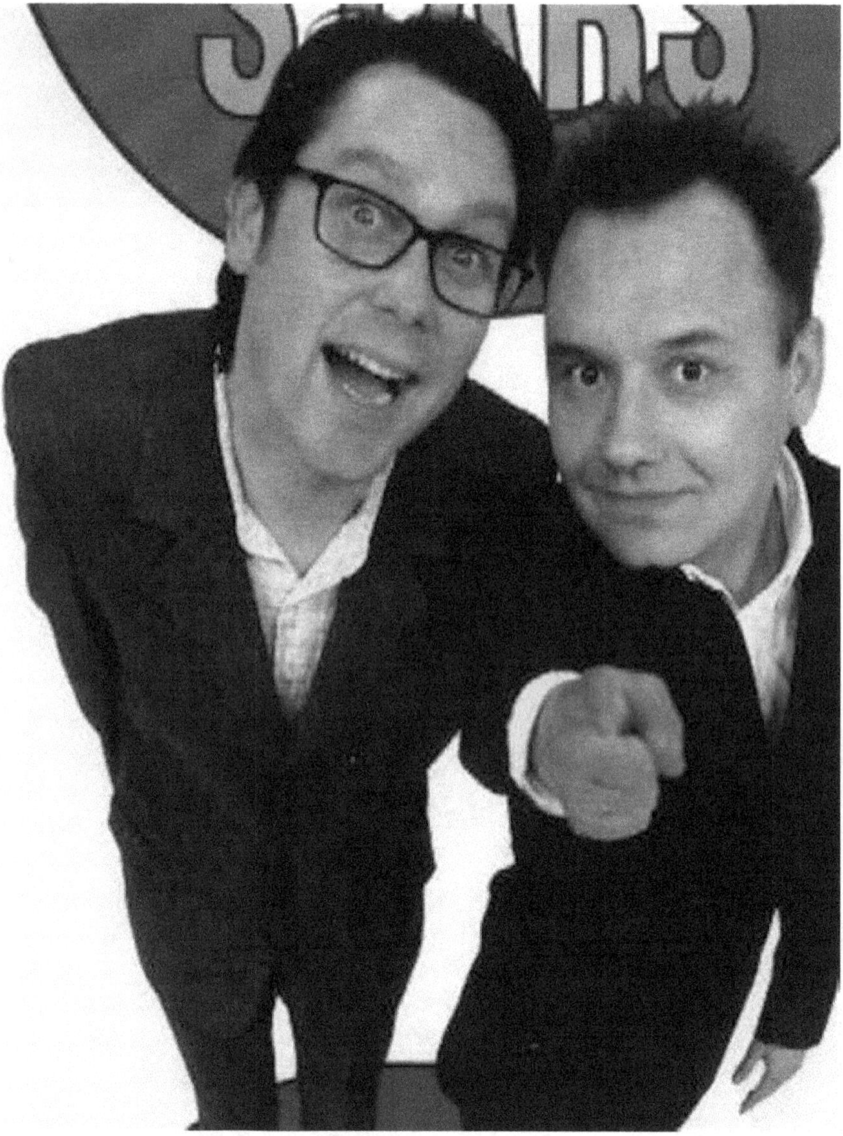

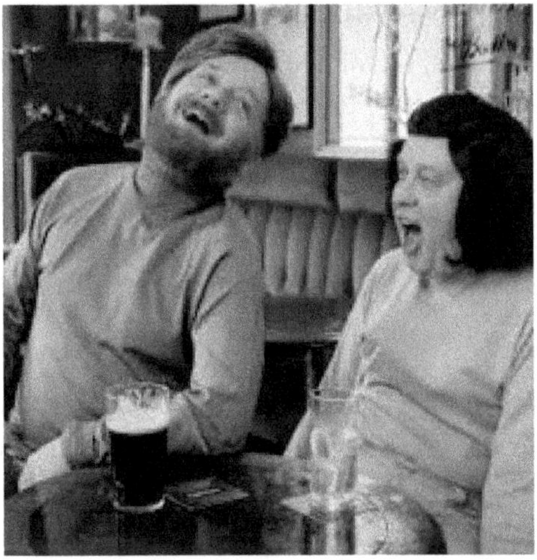

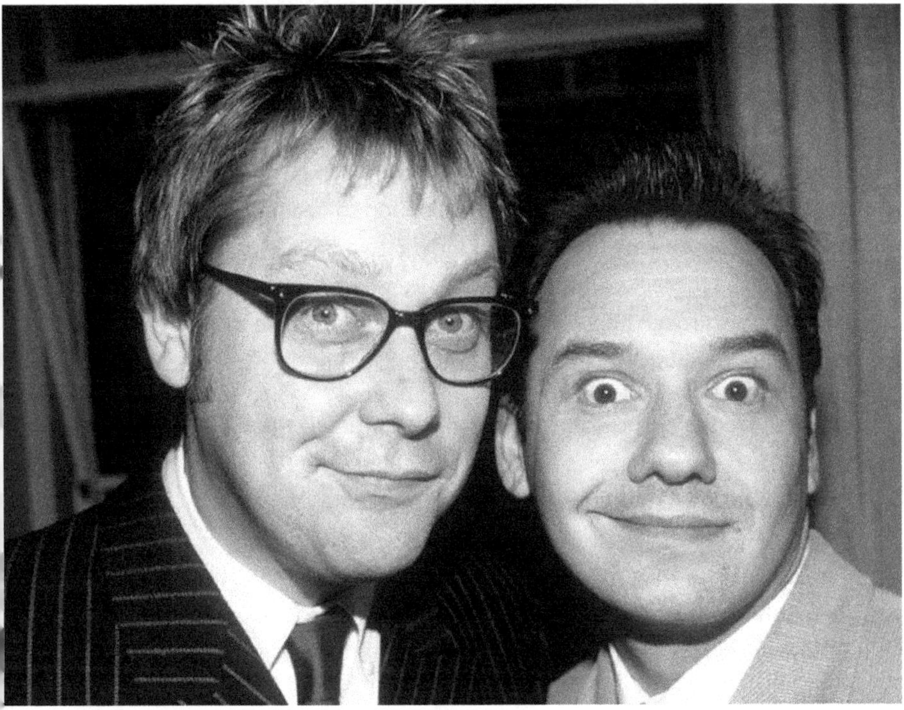

Robert "**Bob**" Renwick **Mortimer**, born on 23rd May 1959, at 9 Tollesby Road, Linthorpe, nr. Middlesbrough, North Riding of Yorkshire, England, UK is a comedian, podcast presenter, and actor, who's best known for his work with Vic Reeves as part of their Vic & Bob comedy double act. Mortimer was brought up with his brothers in the Linthorpe area of Middlesbrough, his father, a biscuit salesman, having died in a car crash when Bob was 7 years old.

Mortimer attended Acklam High School on the site of Acklam Hall in Acklam, Middlesbrough, where his schoolmates included Ali Brownlee, who went on to become a sports presenter on BBC Tees. Bob trialled for local professional association football club Middlesbrough but wasn't able to join the club as a professional due to arthritis, although he still supports them.

He left school with 3 A-levels, going on to study law at the universities of Sussex and Leicester, where Mortimer became involved in political causes and the punk rock movement, starting a group named Dog Dirt. After leaving university with an LLM in Welfare Law, Bob moved to London to become a solicitor for Southwark Council then moved to a private practice in Peckham, where his work with Public Health Act cases regarding cockroach infestation of council properties led to a local paper dubbing Mortimer 'The Cockroach King'.

Bob went to the Goldsmith's Tavern in New Cross, London during 1986, to see a new show by a comedian called Vic Reeves. Mortimer was impressed by the performance, particularly the character Tappy Lappy, Reeves attempting to tap dance while wearing a Bryan Ferry mask and planks on his feet. Bob approached Vic after the show then the pair began writing material for the next week's show together, becoming good friends, while forming a band called the Potter's Wheel. Mortimer began to perform on the show, which was christened Vic Reeves Big Night Out, creating characters including the Singing Lawyer, Graham Lister, Judge Nutmeg and the Man With the Stick.

The show became successful in South London, outgrowing Goldsmith's Tavern, moving to the Albany Empire in Deptford in 1988. Bob soon became an integral part of the performance, having a weekly break from his legal work, which had begun to disillusion him. He said that the final straw was a run in with a mugger, who when recognising Mortimer as having represented him legally, backed off apologising for not realising who he was earlier.

Vic and Bob made their TV debut on the short-lived comedy chat show One Hour with Jonathan Ross during 1989, in the game show segment known as knock down ginger. Late that year, the duo made their first television pilot together, Vic Reeves Big Night Out, which remained true to their nightclub act's variety show format. Mortimer took what was meant to be a 10-week break from his legal job to film the series but never returned.

The pair later created a one-off pilot for a sitcom called The Weekenders in 1992 then the sketch show The Smell of Reeves and Mortimer the following year and Shooting Stars, a comedy panel show that was first broadcast during December 1993. After being commissioned, Shooting Stars ran for 5 series from 1995 - 2002, with a special anniversary edition broadcast in December 2008. A 6th series was broadcast in late 2009, followed by a 7th series during mid-2010 then 8th in 2011.

Vic and Bob appeared in a 2nd sketch show during 1999, titled Bang Bang, It's Reeves and Mortimer then the following year, Mortimer played the part of Jeff Randall in Randall & Hopkirk (Deceased), opposite Reeves as Marty, with Emilia Fox as Jeannie Hurst. Vic and Bob were listed in The Observer as one of the 50 funniest acts in British comedy in 2003. In a poll to find the Comedians' Comedian during 2005, the duo were voted the 9th greatest comedy act of all time by fellow comedians and comedy insiders.

Mortimer played Reeves' hairdresser, Carl, in the weekly BBC Radio 2 sketch show entitled Vic Reeves' House Arrest on 17th November 2007. Vic announced on 27th February the following year that he and Bob were working together on a new sitcom about super heroes who get their powers through a malfunctioning telegraph pole. Reeves and Mortimer filmed episodes of a new BBC sitcom, House of Fools in November 2013, also featuring Matt Berry as Beef, Morgana Robinson as Julie, and Dan Skinner as Bosh.

The pair cancelled the first leg of their live tour, 25 Year of Reeves and Mortimer: The Poignant Moments during October 2015, after Bob underwent an emergency triple heart bypass.

Mortimer and Vic starred in a relaunch and new singular episode of their comedy Big Night Out for the BBC on 29th December 2017, the show having been remade and renamed as Vic and Bob's Big Night Out. The episode remained true to the classic Big Night Out formula, being composed of comedy songs, skits, characters and sketches. It was the first time the Big Night Out series had featured Mortimer's name in the title, a full series of Vic and Bob's Big Night Out having begun on BBC Four in November 2018.

In collaboration with Chris Rea, Mortimer recorded Rea's hit Let's Dance with his favourite football team, Middlesbrough in 1997, the single reaching UK No. 44. Bob appeared in an episode of Mash and Peas with Matt Lucas, David Walliams and Reece Shearsmith during 1996-97, in a sketch spoofing Seinfeld, titled 'I'm Bland... yet all my friends are krazy!'.

Mortimer fought and defeated Les Dennis in July 2002 in the BBC's first Celebrity Boxing match, as part of Sport Relief. Bob presented the Channel 4 list show The 100 Greatest World Cup Moments of All Time! that year. An updated show, again hosted by Mortimer, was broadcast by the channel during 2010, to coincide with the FIFA World Cup finals.

Bob produced and presented the 2nd match, The Fight, a year later, which matched Grant Bovey vs Ricky Gervais. Mortimer hosted his first major TV series without Reeves in 2005, a comedy panel game for BBC 1, titled 29 Minutes of Fame, which featured regular guests including Jo Brand. Bob also voiced the character of Father Nicholas in the animated BBC Three series Popetown that year but the show wasn't broadcast by the channel, due to concern over offending Catholic viewers, although it had a DVD release later in 2005.

Mortimer co-wrote the BBC Three sketch comedy Tittybangbang with Jill Parker, the programme starring Lucy Montgomery and Debbie Chazen, with Tony Way, running for 3 series from 2006 to 2007. Bob has appeared on Never Mind the Buzzcocks on BBC 2 on 4 occasions – during 1996, on Sean Hughes' team; in 2000, on Phill Jupitus's team; during 2008, as a guest team captain then in 2012, as a guest host.

Mortimer appeared on the Sky1 panel show A League of Their Own during April 2010, on Andrew Flintoff's team. Bob wrote his first novel, provisionally titled 'Have Her Over My Hedge (You've Never Trimmed It)', with Charlie Higson. Mortimer wrote a sitcom for the BBC starring Mackenzie Crook and Iain Lee. Bob has been a regular guest panelist on the quiz show Would I Lie to You? on BBC 1 since 2012, appearing in episodes broadcast during May 2012, June 2013, September 2014, August 2015, September 2017, December 2017, May 2018, October 2018, and December 2019.

Mortimer appeared on an episode of Ross Noble Freewheeling in November 2013, having also starred as Frank in the E4 comedy Drifters that year. Bob appeared on an episode of the Dave show Alan Davies: As Yet Untitled on 18th June 2014. He was a contestant on Let's Play Darts on 4th March 2015, but lost out to Roisin Conaty then appeared in an episode of Celebrity Squares alongside Vic Reeves that year.

Mortimer took over from the late Rik Mayall as Bombardier Bedford during April 2015, the mascot of Well's Bombardier Beer. Bob has co-hosted a regular podcast, Athletico Mince alongside Andy Dawson since March the following year. He's appeared on many episodes of the Sky1 comedy panel game Duck Quacks Don't Echo. Mortimer won series 5 of Taskmaster in 2017, beating Aisling Bea, Sally Phillips, Nish Kumar and Mark Watson. Bob then competed in the Taskmaster: Champion of Champions series that year against Noel Fielding, Josh Widdicombe, Katherine Ryan and Rob Beckett, coming last.

He teamed up with his long time friend and fellow comedian Paul Whitehouse during June - July 2018 in a BBC2 6 part comedy series, Mortimer & Whitehouse: Gone Fishing. The pair, who've both suffered from heart conditions, shared their thoughts and experiences while fishing at locations around the UK. Bob was a guest on the BBC Radio programme Desert Island Discs on 3rd February 2019, having also appeared on an episode of Travel Man that year.

Mortimer accidentally burnt down his family's home with a firework when he was 7 years old. He's had rheumatoid arthritis over recent years, which gives him great pain when he's stressed, especially before making a TV series or embarking on a tour, Bob controlling the illness with steroids. It was revealed in October 2015 that he was recovering from a triple bypass surgery, which led to the cancellation of the first leg of the Reeves and Mortimer 25 years tour. Bob wed his partner of 22 years, Lisa Matthews that month, the couple, who have two sons, Harry and Tom, live in London. He's a lifelong fan of Middlesbrough Football Club and the rock group Free. Mortimer has been a long-time patron and ambassador for Cats Protection, the UK's leading cat welfare charity (cats.org.uk)

Works and roles

Vic Reeves Big Night Out

The Weekenders

Catterick

The Smell of Reeves and Mortimer

Bang, Bang, It's Reeves and Mortimer

Shooting Stars

Families at War

Randall and Hopkirk (Deceased)

29 Minutes of Fame

Monkey Trousers

House of Fools

'Vic and Bobs Big Night Out' Athletico Mince

Mortimer & Whitehouse: Gone Fishing

How had Bob Mortimer's childhood influenced his attitude to money and his work ethic?

"I was the youngest of 4 boys, raised in North Yorkshire. I was just a toddler when my dad died in a car crash. With my mum, Eunice, being a young widow with a large family, she really struggled money-wise. She worked for the Ministry of Food, going around the country teaching people how to make do with their rations. At Christmas I'd help her count up all her Embassy cigarette coupons and send those off, which would pay for our turkey and Christmas presents. Then, to make things worse, I accidentally burnt our house down when I was 7 – and Mum hadn't insured it. It was devastating for us. We were split up and lived with various relatives for a while. We did eventually return to the house, but it financially crippled her".

What was Bob's first job after graduating from university?

"Binman. Before doing my master's degree in welfare law I took a summer job as a binman, but loved it so much that I stayed for 18 months. I was paid £24.48 / week, which seemed a fortune to me at the time in the early '80s, but I was still young".

Had Mortimer ever worried about making ends meet?

"Yes, when I took my first solicitor's job as in-house legal counsel at Southwark Council. I was a big Left-winger in those days and I was helping the council mount a legal challenge to the Tory government's new poll tax. It was my first time living in London and I was shocked at how expensive it was. I had to go to see the town clerk, who was the boss of the legal department, to tell him I didn't think I could afford to live. He told me about a nearby homeless hostel where I could stay until I got on my feet. I ended up staying there for 3 years".

Was Bob a saver or a spender?

"I spend a lot of money on the little things that make me happy, like £3 falafels from M&S to eat on the train on the way up to Edinburgh, but I do keep a close eye on the bigger picture. I don't flash the cash ridiculously on expensive things. I spend what I get and if I think I'm running out, I do more work. I get tremendous pleasure out of helping my children get on their feet. I paid my son's water bill the other day and that made me strangely happy".

What was the biggest lesson Mortimer had learnt about money?

"Spend what you've got and enjoy doing so, but no more. I don't believe in credit or loans. If Jim [Vic Reeves] and I do a show and I get, say £50,000, I know I've got to make that last".

What did Bob hate about money?

"I hide from all financial matters. I hate receiving letters from utility companies, the taxman and so on, because I automatically assume it's bad news. I don't open them, so somewhere down the line someone knocks on my door from a collections agency or the bailiffs".

What had been Mortimer's worst business decision?

"In my mid-30s everyone was telling me that I had to get myself a pension, because at that time you could have 7 years' worth of your pension allowance in one go, but I had to do it that year or I'd miss out. I saw a statement for the fund the other day and 20 years on I'd made the princely sum of £87".

What had been Bob's best business decision?

"Never putting another penny into my blasted pension! I'm very suspicious of pensions and it makes me uneasy that the Government really pushes them. I don't trust their motivation. However, pensions were playing on my mind two years ago when my wife told me I should make other plans. So I bought shares in online clothing retailer Boohoo.com, because I saw how popular the site was with my teenagers and their friends. Previously I'd invested in IQE, a Welsh technology firm that makes semiconductors and all the precise internal guts of the iPhone, among other things. I bought into them when they were just penny shares but they're now around 162p".

What was the one change Mortimer would make in the business or financial world?

"Raise the minimum wage so that people in service jobs can survive, not just exist. I don't know what the consequences would be, but it feels like the right thing to do".

Did Bob use a financial adviser?

"No, I think it must have been something I picked up from my extended family. I'm not disrespecting it as a profession, but there's something in me that doesn't believe a word they say. I know I'm probably missing out, but when I see all these questionable offshore trusts it doesn't help my suspicions".

Why did Mortimer support Cats Protection?

"We have two cats, Mavis and Goodmonson that provide endless entertainment and companionship. Cats Protection do a tremendous job in very sad situations, taking in strays or unwanted cats, rehabilitating them then rehoming them".

Did Bob have any financial concerns as he was getting older?

"Thankfully, I own our house in London. If we didn't, I'd worry".

What financial advice had Mortimer passed on to his children?

"I told both of them to open an Isa and I know one of them definitely has. There's an app called Moneybox and when you register for it they open an Isa for you and whenever you make a purchase on a card they round it up to the next pound and put the difference into your Isa. It may not seem like much, but it's part of getting into the regular habit of saving".

The 10 most surprising truths from the guests on Would I Lie to You? including the celeb that went to school with Bin Laden & Mel Giedroyc's cheeky snog

1. Dom Joly went to school with Osama bin Laden.

It was a Christian Quaker school in Lebanon for children between the ages of 4 and 18. They weren't friends because they were at different ends of the age spectrum. Joly said he didn't think the Quaker teaching 'sat very well' with Bin Laden.

2. When he was 7 years old, Bob Mortimer set fire to his house with a box of fireworks.

"Left alone one afternoon, he lit a sparkler, the sparks falling into a box of fireworks. As the box began to sizzle he carried it to the kitchen and threw it in, not realising that he'd dropped one firework on the way. This engulfed the living room in flames then the entire house was destroyed. When he was asked why he didn't take the burning fireworks outside he replied, "Mum said don't go out!"

3. Mel Giedroyc once had a snog with another guest appearing on the same episode of Would I Lie to You? It was Dermot O'Leary, having happened at the end of 'Late Lunch', a series they were working on during 1998. Dermot said that he couldn't remember if he'd been in another relationship at the time of the kiss, although Mel assured him that he told her he was single.

4. Richard Osman once buried a badger with The Banker from Deal or No Deal.

They'd become friends during Richard's time as a producer on the programme, being on holiday together in Cornwall when their car hit and killed the animal. The Banker's wife insisted that they return to the house, get spades, go back to bury the badger then say a few words".

5. Patrick Kielty punched Muhammad Ali in the face in 2004, drawing blood from his nose.

Kielty had been invited to Ali's hotel room in Dublin after introducing him on stage at a sports event the night before. The two were stage-fighting for a photo, when Patrick thought Ali was about to lean back but he moved forward just as Kielty threw the punch. A hasty retreat was sensibly made by the blond comic.

6. Ricky Tomlinson accidentally convinced somebody not to join The Beatles.

Ricky once persuaded the pianist John Duff Lowe to leave an early incarnation of the Beatles, named the Quarrymen, to join his own band, Hobo Rick and the City Slickers, after a fellow member spotted Lowe, said he was great then suggested that they should poach him".

7. Kevin Bridges once accidentally bought a horse.

He was on holiday with a pal in Bulgaria, the pair believing that they were renting it for a ride for 25 minutes but for £90 they'd bought a friend for life.

8. Katherine Parkinson thought that the Wombles were real

When Katherine sat her biology GCSE exam, a question came up asking for 3 examples of mammals. She wrote 'bear, whale and womble', thinking that The Wombles, although not a documentary, was actually based on real-life creatures but it didn't do much damage, as she still got an A.

9. Steve Jones saved P Diddy from drowning when they were in St Tropez.

The two of them had been invited onto a boat owned by a mutual friend c. 2010, when Steve saw the rapper sailing around in the water. He dived in, brought him back to the boat then got a simple "thanks man" from the star.

10. Charles Dance once had a chimpanzee to his house for tea.

It was sent on ahead by a friend who was running late. He tried to give it Marmite on toast, but the guest wasn't impressed — cheese and tomato ones went down much better. When asked why his friend had a chimp, Dance said she had "very few friends".

Vic Reeves starred in a new comedy sketch show for Radio 2, which paired him up with his old partner, Bob Mortimer, for the first time in 6 years. Noel Fielding, from The Mighty Boosh, and Nancy Sorrell also starred. On each show Vic was put under house arrest for a wacky crime he hadn't committed then followed his attempts to alleviate the boredom of his captivity through a variety of highly unusual tasks and events.

Episode 1 - Saturday 16th November

Reeves tried to wake up the street in a slightly unusual manner, attempting to dress his pet walrus in some party gear, listening to his unusual record collection then trying to play The Legendary Stardust Cowboy. Vic also hoped to enter The X Factor with a distinctly alternative way of singing a Kylie Minogue hit in the bath; watched a bizarre American sitcom on TV; tried to have his hair cut by his hairdresser, Carl, played by Bob Mortimer then helped a vagrant who was looking for work, played by Noel Fielding, with the help of a few sausages.

Episode 2 - Saturday 24th November

Whilst holed up at home, Reeves woke the street up with the help of a cannon, once again frustrating the local vicar. He gave work to a local vagrant played by Noel Fielding, which this week involved Vic's birds, and watched a terrible TV quiz show. Carl the hairdresser, played by Bob Mortimer, tried to cut Vic's hair but became bogged down by danger in Reeves's garden.

Vic also listened to an Anthony Newley classic from his record collection but needed a peacock to help him play it; tried to put a tuxedo on his pet alligator then valiantly tried to enter The X Factor by singing a Julie Andrews classic in the bath. As ever, a day in the life if Reeves was home was a wholly unpredictable one.

Episode 3 - Saturday 1st December

To keep himself busy, Vic helped the local vagrant with some work involving potatoes. He also watched a particularly unusual TV cookery show with Davey Stott, had a visit from Carl the hairdresser (Bob Mortimer), who tried to cut Reeves's hair but was put off by a mystery smell in the house. Vic had problems playing one of his records by the legendary Mrs Miller from his record collection; he tried to dress his pet pig in a new pair of trousers, with disastrous results then tried his hand at entering The X Factor by singing a Kylie classic in the bath.

Episode 4 - Saturday 8th December

Reeves woke up the street with a bit of help from a chainsaw or two. The local vagrant helped Vic out then tried to dissect a mammal. Reeves watched a very unusual TV edition of Superman featuring a character from Coronation Street. Carl the hairdresser (Bob Mortimer) tried to cut Vic's hair, who then had problems listening to one of the records from his vast collection, which that week featured an actor from Star Trek. Reeves also got into trouble with his pet monkey, before once again trying to get onto The X-Factor, by singing a Sinatra classic.

Episode 5 - Saturday 15th December

Vic once again woke up under House Arrest for a crime he hadn't committed, which that week involved Bruce Forsyth. Reeves began the day by waking up the street with a bit of help from his extensive drum collection, once more annoying the local vicar. He also helped a vagrant then watched a very odd Noel Coward-style movie on TV.

Carl the hairdresser (Bob Mortimer) tried to cut Vic's hair but became paranoid about possible torture devices. Reeves also tried to fill the time by listening to one of his more unusual records, but was foiled by it jumping, having to resort to extreme measures, as yet again, it was an incident-filled day at home for Vic, with never a dull moment.

Episode 6 - Saturday 22nd December

In the last episode of the series, Reeves woke up the street with the aid of a few rockets, leading to a minor war with the local vicar. He also helped the local vagrant with some work, which involved the Moon and some pelicans. After watching a truly boring sports show on TV he tried to have his hair cut by Carl the hairdresser (Bob Mortimer), but a strange tale was told instead.

To help pass the time, Vic also tried to play a Bobby Darin record but was thwarted, so tried to clothe his pet elephant with a neck tie – with disastrous results. In his final attempt to get on The X Factor, he then sang the classic Barbra Streisand/Neil Diamond song, You Don't Bring Me Flowers.

Vic Reeves put himself at the mercy of a man with a cut throat razor when he enjoyed a Big Day Out in the North East. Reeves, who was brought up in Darlington, made a whistle-stop tour of the area to meet apprentices working in roles ranging from gentlemen's grooming to cooking and car restoration. As a former mechanical engineering apprentice in Newton Aycliffe during the '70s, Vic was on the road to support the Learning and Skills Council's Apprenticeship Week, which reunited him with his former trainer David Allison at the National Railway Museum in Shildon.

"I'd not seen him for 30 years. He hasn't changed at all. We had a good chat and he asked me if I wanted to come back in July for their awards. I actually won the Best Log Book of the Year Award when I was an apprentice," said Reeves. The comedian, whose TV shows ranged from Vic Reeves' Big Night Out to Shooting Stars, may not have had a career in mechanical engineering but he reckoned his apprenticeship wasn't wasted. "I did it, I went through it and it was good. It's still useful, I still use the skills I learned around the house."

During his visit, Vic said he and his comedy partner Bob Mortimer were keen to resurrect one of their most popular TV shows, while also having plans for a new comedy. "We might be doing Shooting Stars again – it depends on the BBC. We're also working on a sitcom. It's about super heroes who get skills through a telegraph pole that malfunctions then they go around helping people in their local community," he said. Reeves finished his tour by working with hospitality and catering apprentice Dan Sullivan at the Travelling Man pub at West Boldon, where he helped to cook lunch.

Bob Mortimer came so close to death that he was given special permission to marry his partner of 22 years Lisa Matthews in the morning, just 1/2 hr before undergoing a triple heart bypass operation. Bob's comedy partner Vic Reeves wasn't at the last minute wedding, just before he went under the surgeon's knife. The comedian had been told the previous autumn that he needed surgery because his arteries were 95% blocked.

Couples are usually required to give 28 days' notice to their local register office before the ceremony, but special dispensation can be granted if the bride or groom is suffering from a terminal illness or has an operation for a serious illness scheduled. Mortimer, 56, said: "I found out on the Thursday that I needed surgery, so I made a will on the Friday. My consultant said I was incredibly ill, so the registrar in London gave me permission to get married on the Monday. So I got married at 9.30am on the Monday then went to hospital at 10am to have my operation".

Vic didn't have the chance to be his best man, because the only guests at the ceremony were the couple's two children, Harry and Tom. The news of his heart problems "came completely out of the blue" after visiting the doctor with a suspected chest infection, he said. The stars of slapstick BBC sitcom House of Fools toured live later that year. Speaking ahead of the 25 Years of Reeves & Mortimer tour, the first leg of which had to be cancelled that October because of the operation, the comedian said:

"I feel fine. We're doing a little warm-up show on Saturday ... If I don't drop we'll be fine. I've just redone all my tests and they said if I was a builder or a scaffolder I would be absolutely fine to do it and we don't do anything like heavy labour in the show". Bob still had to monitor his health, with a device that gave a constant reading of his heart rate. If it went above a certain limit, he'd have to stop the show.

Mortimer labelled the series of shows a "nostalgia tour", which featured characters from across the double act's comedy career. The tour was their first since 'Weathercock 1495', back in 1995. Vic said: "We've been thinking about it for some time -

shall we go on tour? Because we're quite happy making films but we thought: " It's about time". The 15-date tour began in Leeds on January 30th then finished in London on February 16th.

Bob Mortimer spoke about his battle against rheumatoid arthritis, a disease from which his mother also suffered. The 42-year-old revealed that he'd been left in "absolute agony" when the condition, which affects much of his body, spread to his eye. Bob said: "I have to be careful, because I have rheumatoid arthritis all over my body. Steroids keep it under control its treatable, but not curable, flaring up in a major attack every now and then. The doctors can only give you steroids and statistics, such as theres a 1-in-10 chance youll end up in a wheelchair.

My mum is crippled with it. Whenever I do a show, theres a price to pay. Ive recently started to suffer from iritis, which is when it attacks the iris of the eye. It's absolute agony, but Im not going to give in to it". On making a living from comedy, Mortimer said: "What a great way to earn money throwing jokes at each other across the living room. I was a solicitor once, so Im truly grateful, because I know what its like to have a proper job.

I eat a tin of sardines every day. I had one just a few minutes ago. Kippers or smoked haddock are a nice treat. I have quite a thing about having a fish on its own on the plate. Before we did

Gone Fishing, Paul Whitehouse and I sort of knew that 'heart' would become a bit of a label for us [Mortimer had a triple bypass during 2015; Whitehouse had stents fitted that same year]. Now we get so many tweets about people who've made their dad get their heart checked. We have a lot of other ailments but I expect we probably won't talk about them as much.

Dad died in a car accident when I was 6. I've since discovered that in situations like that, one of the children – often the youngest, like me – will take on the role of 'hero child'. Not out of any grand gesture necessarily, it just tends to happen. I'd peel spuds, top and tail gooseberries, dish out tripe and generally be Mum's kitchen helper. She often said: 'If you can't cook eggs, Robert, you can't be a chef'. My scrambled, especially, are very good.

I used to like getting cups then putting tiny bits of food and liquids in them. I'd grow mould plumes in the dark wardrobe of my little back bedroom. Not to eat them, mind – just to admire the growing power. On the way to fishing, I'll pick up my pocket meats and a lump of cheese – all the things I'm not meant to eat

Mum was a cook for most of her life. During the war, she'd been with the Ministry of Food, going around the country showing people how to best use egg powder. That frugality lasted – I remember as a kid, when we visited the butcher she'd often ask for lots of 'bacon bones'. In the 1950s, my mum ran hotels with my dad – him doing admin, her the food. I've sat outside a few pubs they ran, like the Bell Inn in Epping, and wondered about them working together. After Dad died, Mum was teaching cookery at a secondary school. She'd cook all day, so didn't really want to cook again for 4 boys when she returned home knackered.

I once accidentally set fire, with a sparkler, to a box of fireworks then threw them from the living room into Mum's kitchen. They scorched the Formica and the lino, so I got down on my hands and knees, crying, to clean the marks with a Brillo pad, then half an hour later walked back into the living room, which was ablaze. You'd think you'd get a right rollicking from Mum for burning the house down, but it was too desperate a situation, so her priority was not to shout at me at all.

When I went fishing with mates as a kid I'd usually have strawberry jam or banana sandwiches on Mother's Pride with sugar sprinkled all over. At one point I was putting 17 sugars in my tea. I know it's unbelievable and I do wonder sometimes what my mum was thinking to allow it. The weirdest thing was that if I had 18 teaspoons it was too sweet. I suppose if I was trying to analyse it, losing my dad was more upsetting than I'd have realised, yet I got quite a kick out of sugar.

We tend to head down to Hampshire to fish. I'll set off with no food at all, but on the way down I'll pick up my pocket meats – scotch egg, sausage roll – and a lump of cheese. All the things I'm not meant to eat in my pocket to nibble during the day. Nic Roeg said, 'You can get away, but you can't get away from yourself', but I can look at my watch, expecting 1/2 hr has passed, realising it's been hours. I certainly think in those hours I've got away from myself.

I launched Cadbury's Boost bar. For years and years my mum had asked, 'When are you going to go back to your job as a solicitor?' but once she saw me in Boost adverts she realised I could make a living outside law. They were expensive ads; filmed in the south of Spain with loads of cowboys and a big catering budget. It was lobsters in tents in the middle of a desert, brought to me with sparkling wine.

I can't remember ever cooking food to impress a woman. The idea's quite cheesy and sort of makes my skin crawl but I sometimes make a special effort to impress my cats, with chicken liver or something. It's tricky to know if a cat's impressed. They might give me a little look, a glimpse at least. That's cat ownership for you.

There's lots of food in the new series of Big Night Out. We have a hotdog sausage, its appearance activated by buzzer, which we use as a full stop in medical arguments between doctors. We've often used slices of white bread as facial disguise, with holes for our eyes. It's benign, because no one wearing bread means you terrible harm. We look for items, often food, which have a benign feeling, corned beef, for instance, seeming very useful for what we do. In the last series we ate a whole can while sexy music played.

I got married at a registry office, at 9 o'clock in the morning, but was crying during the ceremony. I had to be at hospital at 10.30am for my heart op, so we had time to go for a great big cafe fry-up, meant to be my last, although it hasn't been, if truth be known. When I arrived at the hospital the nurses presented me with a big chocolate cake as a wedding present. I thought it a little odd on a heart ward, but my old pipes were about to go, so there was no point being kind to them.

I always put prunes in my salads, or pears, water chestnuts, celery, those sorts of stringy foods. I'm not trying to be scientific, but I've been told by the experts who look after me that the body uses bad cholesterol to digest that stuff then you shoot out your bad cholesterol, basically. Happy days. In my kitchen is an old-fashioned sweet jar with a cow's heart in it, with an arrow through it. It was given to me as a gift after my operation. The blood red of a heart and the chrome silver of the arrow are a useful reminder of the damage you could do to your heart in a kitchen.

Because of heart disease I should avoid steak and kidney pie and stilton cheese, which is about # 3 in cheeses with the highest amount of fat but if I was talking honestly, either would be my favourite.

A 3-egg omelette, / person, with 1 1/2 egg shells of milk, 1/2 a shell of butter, in a hot pan with a bit of lard. Push it away, then pull it back. If you don't like it runny in the middle I'll pop it under the grill for 30 secs.

The Cleveland Tontine, next to the A19. An unassuming looking, but extraordinary place; its black puddings are brought over from a French market. One of the only places I've eaten what couldn't be recreated by Mum.

Just minutes into an interview with Vic Reeves and Bob Mortimer, the latter requested a plate of "really childish" biscuits to go with his cup of tea. A Jammie Dodger? A Penguin? "The ones with pink on, party rings!", said Reeves. Proffered a plate of chocolate bourbons, the duo leant in to inspect the selection closely. Following a tense pause Vic said, sagely: "That's quite an adult biscuit, that". That the duo would've preferred something a little more whimsical, even in biscuit form, wasn't surprising, known as they were for their cartoonish brand of comedy.

The pair had worked together for over 30 years after meeting in a pub in south London. Their latest offering was a new 4-part series of Vic and Bob's Big Night Out, which had been brought back by the BBC the previous year after first being broadcast on Channel 4 as Vic Reeves' Big Night Out for two series in 1990. The show was being billed as an 'hilarious 1/2 hr of mischief and mayhem', featuring skits, stunts and songs all performed in front of a live audience at breakneck pace.

Indeed, it was so quick that the pair were usually home by 9pm: "It used to be get down the pub for 9pm, but now it's getting home," said Reeves. "That's the old age speaking. It's a nice discipline, I wish we'd thought of it when we were younger," said Mortimer. When they were younger their anarchic strand of comedy had been much more prevalent: "Everyone was doing it, Tommy Cooper, Spike Milligan. That's what a comedian was," said Bob.

Nowadays it was wryly observational stand-ups who were selling out arenas, while easy-going sitcoms populated TV listings. The pair though, were frank about the situation, conceding that their comedy wasn't the easiest to watch. "There's a lot going on, I've total empathy with people who say: 'Oh f**k this!' then turn off after a couple of minutes".

The duo's first TV show had come about when Michael Grade and Alan Yentob saw the pair perform at a theatre in Deptford. "They saw it then said: 'Well, I want that on TV'," said Vic. It wasn't long before they were on Channel 4. "We had the ultimate amount of freedom," he added. Not much had changed since. "The new series is what we've always done, filmed from a different angle," said Reeves. Which angle was that? "Left," he deadpanned.

Technological changes had come and gone, with some more welcome than others. In the early days, the pair would write out their scripts by hand then post them to producers. They recalled fondly the day they'd got their first fax machine in an office they shared with Jools Holland. "We thought: we're into the future now," said Vic. The friends used to feed fruit into the machine to see what would happen: "There's a big black mark [on one of the scripts] and it says: 'Plum here!' because we pushed a plum into it!".

Only Reeves and Mortimer would've thought of faxing fruit but one couldn't help but wonder whether routines like theirs, with their slapstick sketches and silly songs, would still be commissioned. "I'm not sure it would. It's a lot more strict; you have to do exams and everything now," said Vic. The pair didn't watch much comedy themselves but Bob was a fan of the US Office, while Reeves watched Brooklyn Nine-Nine.

"I do give the new British comedies a quick glance but if it doesn't grab me straight away…" Vic trailed off. Commissioners have become safer, suggested Mortimer, with the same shows churned out ad nauseam. "The new sitcoms that are successful are just the same as the old ones but they swear their f**king heads off!" The duo's own sitcom, the surreal House of Fools, ran for two series during 2014 then 2015.

"I can't remember why we decided to do it," said Bob. "Someone will have said: 'Have you ever thought of doing a sitcom?' and we've gone: 'Yeah, all right. It's just a tool really, it's just the end of a paintbrush. It's the same stuff," said Reeves. Had they been frustrated when it was dropped? Mortimer thought it was a money thing, British drama selling across the globe, but not comedy, although Vic had another theory: "Whatever we've done seems to get just two series. I don't know if it's a plot by the BBC to make us think of something new".

Unlike many other comedians, Reeves and Bob's work wasn't driven by what was going on externally. In a world where the power of satire had been annulled by the ridiculousness of the real world, their music hall act had become timeless, not being influenced by the events of Brexit nor the latest actions of Donald Trump, being all the better for it.

"I think there's a lovely space, which is: honestly, it's just a laugh. You don't have to know who's in power, or what's happening, you don't have to imagine the stereotype, it's just for the pure delight of it," said Mortimer. The secret to their success, though, was surely their relationship, the pair saying that they never rowed?: "Everyone wants to know that. They say people who do comedy are depressed clowns, but we're not depressed either," said Vic.

Bob thought that their double act worked because neither of them had an ounce of ego, while Reeves said it was because they'd developed a psychic connection. "It makes it even easier – and what we're looking for is the easiest passage through life". However, there may've been a new partnership in town, in a series with Paul Whitehouse, Mortimer & Whitehouse: Gone Fishing, in which the pair chatted amiably about life while fishing, having been recommissioned for a 2nd series.

It was a gentle, warm-hearted show, which was as much about male friendship as it was about pike. Was Reeves jealous? He didn't take the bait: "Not at all, we've always done separate things," Vic said, coming up with an idea for the next series. "Have you ever suggested, for a laugh, hooking up an old bicycle or a welly?" Bob was rather more thoughtful. "I don't think I'd have done a comedy show with someone else, but doing a bit of fishing… that's all right".

The pair had no plans to slow down, Mortimer being in good health after his triple heart bypass in 2015, which postponed the pair's reunion tour. "I packed in smoking and I don't eat as much fat. I miss them terribly," Bob said. He'd become "hyper-sensitive" to his heart, he said, noticing each time it did "weird things". Reeves suggested that he have a glass panel fitted in his chest so he could check it every now and again but getting older had given Mortimer pause for thought: "Average I've got about 12 years left," he said, gesturing with a chocolate bourbon. "So you start thinking… that's 3 more World Cups".

Bob Mortimer and Paul Whitehouse accidentally stayed in a 'sex pub,' while making their BBC 2 fishing show. In a spin-off book, the pair revealed that they booked the unusual accommodation following the advice of 76-year-old angler and TV presenter John Bailey, when they were shooting an episode about catching pike in Norfolk. Paul said it looked lovely, but 'a little alarm bell went off,' when they found a sauna in one of the rooms.

Bob said: "I had a walk around and at the end of the corridor was a big door with one of those yellow plastic signs outside, like they put out when the floor gets wet but it didn't have a slippery floor warning on it. It said, 'Don't come in — kissing and cuddling going on here', so I looked through the smoked glass window on the door and there was a hot tub, which I believe, was full of couples having it off".

Whitehouse thought that the clientele was also a lot younger than the average countryside B&B. "We went down the next morning — and you know how in rural hotels at breakfast there's always old couples? Not one. Just me and him. The two of us came down to breakfast and waved to them all, 'Good morning! What are you up to today? Group sex? Right-o! No, that's very kind, but we're going pike fishing! Better put the old thermals on!".

"This is the tale of Murray Sterling..." sang Bob Mortimer in a faux-Scottish accent that was one part Mel Gibson in Braveheart and 3 parts Groundskeeper Willie from the Simpsons. "His 18th birthday was fast approaching, and he knew he must escape the clutches of the island before that date, or he'd be forced to spend the rest of his adult life in the caves 'neath the island, digging for precious stones to adorn the Laird's numerous ceremonial capes and bongos".

Mortimer was in Athletico Mince, a podcast co-created and co-hosted by Bob and Andy Dawson, which from episode 1 of 38 had derailed from its intended topic of football, having become a bizarre and engrossing world of idle chat, improvised tales and sketches that often prolapsed mid-joke. In this odd world, former England football manager Steve McLaren was a carpet salesman who drove a clown car, owning a sensitive yellow snake named Casper who vomited everywhere. In another story, ex-footballer Michael Owen tried to open a restaurant called ISIS. At the end of each episode, Mortimer finished by singing a 'Scottish song' about life on a strange and magical island similar to The Wicker Man's 'Summerisle'. The show had already reached 4.4 million listens.

It wasn't unusual territory for Bob – or, at least, strange territory was where he felt most at home. He and his life-long writing partner Vic Reeves had kickstarted a golden age of British TV comedy, which had started with the birth of their flagship show, Big Night Out, in 1990, ending shortly after Ricky Gervais' The Office. They were nonsensical, irreverent and intensely northern at all times, their surreal sketches ranging from turning the pop star Morrissey into a monkey who reviewed electrical appliances, to making Masterchef's Lloyd Grossman a floating Frankenstein with cutlery for fingers.

Their quiz show Shooting Stars, which at its height pulled in over 6 million viewers / week, once blessed a mainstream TV audience with the sight of a confused Larry Hagman from Dallas being presented with a 'Fartridge' - half fart, half partridge. If other comedians of their generation held up a mirror to society, then Mortimer and Reeves held up a watercolour painting of Sylvester Stallone staring at a potato.

While Vic had gone on to present documentaries, stage art exhibitions and written books, Bob remained something of an enigma. Apart from a few panel show appearances and some writing, he hadn't really courted solo fame, getting an interview taking 6 months of him wondering why the hell anyone would want to speak to him. Not many folk knew much about his life, but 30 years after he'd first appeared on TV, his creativity was still quietly pumping like an understated garden fountain.

One sunny September morning Mortimer was at his manager's office in Fitzrovia, London after trying to buy football tickets for the next Middlesbrough away game. There was a cheeky boyish look in his eye, belying his 57 years, like he'd come from putting cling film over a toilet or pulling someone's trousers down. Bob pulled out a vape, took a long, deep inhale then began talking.

"That's the thing, you see, we were never good enough to write proper punchlines. Non sequiturs and that, we can write all f*cking day but bringing things to a conclusion isn't easy". Non sequiturs flowed out of Mortimer like tea bags from a courthouse. It was very easy to write them but almost impossible to write them funnily. A tweet he'd posted the previous August, had over 1,000 likes: "Just back from 2km run... top hat fell off twice but was easily recovered using my dancing cane. #sweetcorn."

Why was it funny? One couldn't deconstruct it or imitate it, it often not making sense, but deep down one knew that it was, somehow, very funny. In an age of anger and despair, with the proliferation of politics and seriousness through nearly every realm of life, comedy with an otherworldly nonsense to it would no doubt remain popular.

"The more cynical commentators on our careers would say that the northern accent has been the basis of our success. There was a certain authenticity to the voice, which isn't to my credit; I was just born there. Whenever I go back to Middlesbrough now, it always hits me immediately how f,*cking obsessed people are at making you laugh up there. Obsessed so much it can get on your tits. I think there's something in that, in being from the north. It's a real currency. I think the people in the north are genuinely lovely. I know amongst them there are Brexiters, twats and violent people, but in a very general way, I think they're lovely. You can take the piss out of a Geordie and he's absolutely fine with it," said Bob.

After graduating from the University of Sussex with a law degree, he'd no idea what his next step might be, leaving the north for 3 years having exposed him to challenges that he hadn't expected. Mortimer experienced bouts of depression, having began to suffer from crippling social anxiety: "It was just, like... f*cking awful. It's like you're walking in a cloud, and life is just sh*t. I came back from university, shyness having basically f*cked up my life. I'd realised I don't work out there in the real world".

Bob moved back home to Middlesbrough, getting a job as a bin man. On his first day, he worked in his local neighbourhood with a man he described as "the hardest man in Middlesbrough, a f*cking beast he was, hell of a size! I remember once a dog bit him under a gate when we were getting the bins. He grabbed the dog, kicked 7 shades of sh*t out of it, put it in the bin then turned it upside down on the front step. I've no idea whether that dog was alive or dead".

As he emptied the bins, Mortimer needed to scream out the name of the truck driver, Archie, to come get the bags he'd collected. "You had to f*cking do it. You had to, in public, scream 'Archie!' There was a rhythm to it. The first time, I remember sweating, thinking: it's gonna be me next that needs to shout 'Archie' but you've got to do it, so I finally screamed it... 'Archie!' and it was fine. My world didn't crumble down, my life didn't fall apart, nobody had a go at me; it was just incidental. That was so liberating for me. From that moment on, I could shout 'Archie!' all over Middlesbrough".

Bob then moved to London, where he spent 9 years working as what he described as a "sh*t solicitor" for Southwark council. One night, a friend took him out for a pint to a pub that was then named The Goldsmiths Tavern in New Cross. In a tiny room upstairs, a drunk Mortimer found Jim Moir, an art student known by his comic name of Vic Reeves, performing. He was wearing a Bryan Ferry mask, tap dancing with planks attached to his feet, in front of an audience of only 4 or 5, all of whom he knew personally. Bob was in awe: "I'd never seen anything like it".

Each night, Vic would let anyone volunteer to stand up then do something during the performance, once asking Mortimer to come up at the end of a joke to present him with a dinner table-sized cheque for £8 million for 'ill kids'. At the age of 31, it was Bob's first ever experience of comedy performance but within days they were writing together, although their work heavily relied on ad-libbing. Each week they performed up to 2 1/2 hrs of comedy together on a Thursday night in the pub, most of which was written between the hours of 5 to 7pm that same day. Their comedy was abstract in form, barely having any structure and never really having punchlines.

Notes were minimal, consisting of things like 'Man with stick, wolf' – the rest happening in the moment. Sketches would begin, peak then simply drift off before ending. In one sketch, the pair wore Sean Connery and Jimmy Hill masks while tossing talcum powder around to a soundtrack of trad jazz, but something about it worked. Mortimer recalled one night when Reeves slowly ate a yoghurt onstage while repeatedly saying, "Mmm, lovely yoghurt!" until a heckler told them to f*ck off.

Many who witnessed it brought their friends the following week, their audience doubling then tripling, so upstairs in the pub became downstairs in the pub, before they moved to a nearby theatre. Jonathan Ross, Jools Holland, Paul Whitehouse, BBC commissioner Alan Yentob and Channel 4 chief executive Michael Grade became regulars in their audience, the duo being unaware that they were auditioning for their future. Within 16 live shows, Vic and Bob were commissioned for national television.

Their TV reign became part of British comic legend. Where many comedians created one or two cult classics in their lifetime, the duo created a whole host of them: The Weekenders; Catterick; The Smell of Reeves and Mortimer; Bang, Bang, It's Reeves and Mortimer; Shooting Stars; Monkey Trousers; and House of Fools becoming some of the weirdest programmes their broadcasters would ever air.

Much like Bob later on Athletico Mince, their characters and comedy were completely detached from reality, except for the occasional celebrity they chose to poke fun at, reality boring them. "We were just f*cking kids, desperately trying to cling onto our childhood," said Mortimer. They'd rather write about a world where everyone was on skis, with folk having "massive f*cking ears"; where all Geordies wore bras, getting aggressive when one pointed them out. "I've wanted that world since I was 6 years old. I mean, imagine if there was at least a little comfortable place you could go to now and then, where everyone sat around in big pointy shoes, talking in high pitched voices, asking, 'How are you today? Lovely to see you, have a cup of tea.' It'd just be a lovely place to go to".

The pair were given a primetime slot on BBC1 on a Saturday evening during 1998; the type of slot that later went to Ant and Dec or The X Factor. The millions of families who tuned in for the first episode witnessed this scene: a boy of c. 15 years old, in a Reebok tracksuit and boxing gloves, punching a garden shed. The camera panned then a studio audience cheered, supporting him frantically. Vic and Bob, in ill-fitting suits, leapt between the punches of the boy and the sways of the shed, shouting that he must punch the shed until it was below the height of an average Alsatian.

The boy punched, kicked and hooked, haymakers hitting the shed, as it swayed then began to fall apart. The camera panned to a seated jury made up of male horse jockeys, who cast a quick vote on whether or not the challenge was successfully completed. "We had millions watching a young lad box a shed... I hope you can understand our sense of how amazing that was," said Mortimer. The show 'Families at War,' wasn't renewed for a 2nd season, but it remained a visionary gameshow comedy: art without compromise.

What would Bob's life have been like if he hadn't met Jim Moir that night in New Cross? "I wonder that occasionally, when I'm on a bus or something. I sit and think, 'F*ck, if I hadn't have gone to that club. F*ck...' Because Jim's a genius. A lot of comedians aren't. They're incredibly clever, incredibly hard working, really gifted or incredible mimics, incredible wordsmiths, but Jim is a f*cking genius. Not being boastful, but I've met loads of people in this industry and occasionally you meet a genius, and he's a genius. It's extraordinary, the content in his head".

In October 2015, just months before he and Reeves were about to go on their anniversary tour together, Mortimer lay still but conscious on a hospital bed in intensive care, strongly considering the possibility that he was going to die. He'd just come out of a triple heart bypass, but was recovering poorly. The doctors had deflated a lung to access his heart during the operation, the subsequent re-inflation having loosened 43 years build up of tar from smoking.

That tar was slowly oozing out of Bob's mouth as a gelatinous black slug, blocking the passage of air, before slithering then dripping down his chin. Helpless, he fixed his gaze on a TV at the other end of the hospital ward, where Middlesbrough were in a penalty shootout with Manchester United, to decide who'd progress to the next round of the League Cup, thinking 'I've got to f*cking hang on, to see if Grant Leadbitter scores this penalty'.

Had Mortimer's near-death experience had any profound effects on him – making him think more seriously about life or his legacy as a comedian? He shook his head. What made Bob sad wasn't that life seemed to be evacuating him like sand through a sieve but the things he'd ignored on a daily basis: his loyal egg cup, stood proudly on the shelf; the tea towel that hung resolutely from his oven.

"Those were the things that really mattered to me, that I really had a connection with. Good honest connections". When his wife was out, he'd whisper to the tea towel "I'm really going to miss you. For one minute, I couldn't give a flying f*ck about life or work or legacy, any of that..." His face straightened,

Mortimer looked me straight in the eye, just for a second, his jocular demeanour looking like it might slip for the first time to reveal a deeply serious man. It was uncomfortable, like seeing your dad get upset for the first time but then it was over. "Although, I do see the tea towel now," Bob said, cracking a school-boy smile, which looked like the dam holding back full-on laughter, "I'm beginning to ignore it again."

"I was born at home, 9 Tollesby Road, in the village of Linthorpe, North Yorkshire, near Middlesborough, the youngest of 4 boys. I was just a toddler and my brothers were 5, 8 and 10 when my dad died, so mum Eunice was left to raise us single-handedly. Mum was far too busy to take us out anywhere, but it was a good place to be young. It was small enough so that like-minded people could find each other.

The fields surrounding our housing estate were like another planet to such a small child. There was a burn with a rope swing then when I learnt to ride a bike it was only a short 10-15 minute bike ride to the beautiful countryside of the Cleveland Hills, Roseberry Topping and Great Ayton. It's an often-overlooked part of the countryside, but it's gorgeous, great for adventures, like going fishing, starting fires, all those things young boys do. Plus, we'd always stop for ice cream. Further afield, daytrips for us would be to Durham "to go someplace lovely" as mum would say, or to Northallerton because there was a Betty's Café.

Mum died in 2008, it was hard coming back to the area. She was on her own and I used to come up to visit her and tie it in with watching my beloved Middlesbrough FC. I still have lots of family in the area; one of my brothers is in Northallerton. I don't think you can ever beat the beauty of the Lake District. I visited some extraordinarily beautiful places for my new show with Paul Whitehouse called Paul and Bob Go Fishing. The Wye Valley, Norfolk and Hampshire were real favourites, but the Lake District holds special memories for me, because it was the first place I visited when I was old enough to go on holiday with friends when I was 15. I used to go every year and camp at Derwent Water near Keswick.

When my boys Harry and Tom (20 and 19) were growing up, every Sunday my wife Lisa and I would take them to Dymchurch and New Romney on the south coast. We'd potter about on the beach then take them to the funfair. Things changed as they became teenagers, with the draw of computers, theme parks and urban living in London. When I think of my children's experiences and their friend's experiences, the countryside is a bit of a mystery to them. My suspicion is that the countryside for a lot of kids only exists in Call of Duty games.

The most evocative piece of music I know is Vaughan Williams' Lark Ascending. I can just envisage the animals, birds and fauna coming alive. It's incredibly soothing and culturally nostalgic. I associate it with the Cleveland Hills and Vic, down the valley near Durham. Vic Reeves and I have been using it for 35 years, as we come on stage to do a live show.

Paul Whitehouse is actually my current outdoors hero. I had no idea he had such a deep knowledge of the countryside and the animals and plants in it. When he was a boy, he'd forged a real bond with his dad down the riverbanks in Wales and the Home Counties. You can't really be in love with fishing without understanding everything around it. I've learnt so much from Paul and he's been very patient teaching me about the fragile ecosystem.

I'm falling back in love with the countryside. I used to think I owned it all when I was a teenager then I neglected it for too many years. Filming all over the countryside for the past few months, I've rediscovered it. I'm seeing it through new eyes, but with a nostalgic familiarity. If I were a British animal, I'd have to be the tench. It's a fish that lives a lovely, lazy life at the bottom of the lake, seemingly sleeping a lot and taking the odd gulp of food that may pass by. It's very hard to catch though, but we did during filming Paul and Bob Go Fishing.

In terms of a land animal, it'd be a cat. I stare at my two cats – Mavis and Goodmonson who are a tabby oriental and a chocolate oriental – jealously every day and think that's the life I want. My wife and I would love to have more rescue cats. Now that Lisa and I are empty-nesters with the boys at uni, we love to head off to the country for the weekend. We recently went to the Cotswolds to celebrate our wedding anniversary, which is also the anniversary of my heart bypass operation. The Cotswolds have a magical, picture story-book quality to them. There's a vintage feel to them that reminds me of my childhood, plus there are really nice hotels, like the Painswick.

There are too many cars clogging up our beautiful villages. When I was with Paul in Stockbridge, Hampshire recently, I thought how wonderful it'd be if there were no cars and it was pedestrianised. It sullies the natural splendour. When you take photographs, all you can see is the cars. There's no easy answer to that. As for whether it should be jam or cream first on a scone – jam first, then cream, simply because it's easier to spread cream on jam than jam on cream and yes, I"m a good scone baker, just like they showed me on Celebrity Bake Off!

"My doctor told me that I'd have had a heart attack on stage. He looked at my tour schedule then said I'd most likely have gone down in Southampton".

The year was 2015, which was shaping up to be a big one for Bob Mortimer. Alongside his comedy partner Vic Reeves, he was all set to embark on a 25th anniversary Poignant Moments tour – celebrating the longevity of a comedy duo who went from upstairs at a pub in New Cross to TV in record time with Big Night Out, having shaped and changed the comedy landscape ever since.

If it wasn't for the impending mammoth tour, playing concert halls across the UK, Mortimer said he'd have ignored the chest pains he was experiencing. It's what men so often do, trained by years of 'manning up' and 'boys don't cry'. Instead, he came face to face with mortality, which shocked him. "When I came home from being told I had to have heart surgery, it felt so dramatic. You think it's over. Heart surgery just sounds... it was weird, the things that would make me cry were my favourite egg cup, my cats," said Bob, at the Union Club in Soho. "4 days later they were cutting me open. I was 95% blocked. It's amazing when you see the pictures, because it's an incredibly resistant organ – if there's a gap it will f*cking push that blood through it".

Mortimer, who turned 60 the following year, was fun, youthful, and entirely unstarry, despite being "dead posh" since he'd left Peckham to live in leafy Tunbridge Wells, having made a full recovery. At his first show after his triple heart bypass, a ramshackle warm-up to test new material at the Leicester Square Theatre, he'd regularly looked at the monitor on his wrist to check his heart rate: "Me and Jim [Moir] watched it going up before the show, as the nerves kicked in!"

The 2nd half of the tour had gone ahead to great acclaim, with the pair being all set to record new episodes of their iconic breakthrough show, Big Night Out, broadcast later that year. "I'm really looking forward to it, because it's f*cking nuts. It's f*cking nonsense! We weren't expecting to get the show. We're certainly not expecting to get a 2nd series, so it really is exactly what we want to do. We did a pilot last year and we put in a spoof of First Dates, just as a nod to the mainstream. This time we asked permission not to do any of that. It could go either way".

First, Bob was appearing in a whole new arena, with a different comedy partner. Mortimer & Whitehouse: Gone Fishing, featured the funnyman alongside fellow comic Paul Whitehouse, visiting rivers around the UK. Two men talking and fishing. That was it. If the show was about anything, it was about male friendship, showing the way emotion was hidden beneath jokes, any excuse to avoid difficult subjects being latched on to – a timely tench interrupting Mortimer's discussion of his triple heart bypass in episode one. However, Bob was serious when he talked of Whitehouse, who had a stent fitted following his own heart scare, lifting him out of his post-op slump.

"Paul brought me out of my malaise. I've always been a bit of a recluse, but I really was after the heart thing, everyone knew. He's an extraordinarily lovely human being, who sort of enticed me out under the guise of fishing. I don't fish but had always wanted to after doing it as a kid. We went fishing for the pleasure, him teaching me to fish. He's very serious about it. I like that. The show's quite authentic. We were fishing in some lovely places. Then me and Paul went to the BBC, saying that we'd had these lovely days and found it really interesting – these two old men, thinking about what is friendship like when you're that age".

How had it compared to the intense friendships of youth? "I look back on my friendships before this and I have great friends, but what that actually equates to is occasionally bumping into them somewhere and maybe going to someone's birthday do and catching up with them. That's not what friendship was when I was younger. It was a right laugh having a friend when I was younger. I found myself fishing with Paul and recapturing a bit of what it was like to have a proper friend. Passing our time together. We're at a crossroads in our lives. We've both been told it's the beginning of the end and it made us think we should do this for telly, because it was interesting," said Mortimer.

Bob's friendship with Whitehouse went right back to Big Night Out's early days. Paul was a friend and painting & decorating partner of Charlie Higson, whose university pal was part of Vic Reeves' gang. Surely Mortimer bared his soul to his old pal Vic Reeves, who he described as "honestly, a f*cking genius", in between writing their madcap, farcical 'nonsense'?

"No. Never. What can I say, it's weird, isn't it? I don't talk to anyone and haven't for 30 years. I mean, I have very close friends – I'm very close to Jim [Vic] and we write most days. If there was a fly on the wall, actually we probably do talk about things, hidden under layers of work and jokes. So I do have this friendship with Jim but it's mixed in with work. There are all hidden subplots. We're actually there to write something – and I suppose me and Paul were there to catch fish. I soon learnt that fishing has nothing to do with catching fish," Bob said, the angling amateur of the partnership.

"The best day we had was for the last show. We don't catch a thing but that didn't matter in the slightest. Instead, the fewer fish, the more talk of ailing health, ageing and why men don't get themselves checked out by doctors. I'm a bit evangelistic, because fellas are such f*ckers for it. I asked the nurse what the typical profile on the ward was, of the heart attack person. She said '55-year-old marathon runner'.

Looking back I realise I was absolutely set for it. I was so tired of an afternoon. I just wish more people were aware of it, because if every bloke when they were 50 went to the doctor and asked for a treadmill test, it would save so many f*cking lives. You get on a treadmill, they moniter you to see how quickly the blood is going in and out of your arteries then they can say, 'You're fine, son' and you can forget about it," said Mortimer.

Bob had a lucky escape and he was filling his time with the things he liked. "I got married before my op, I got a special licence. It's hard not to think about what you might've missed but it's a little bit of a gift as well. Do you like football?" Off he went into reveries about Middlesbrough, play-off disappointments and his lifelong liking for the game. From life and death to something much more important in a heartbeat...

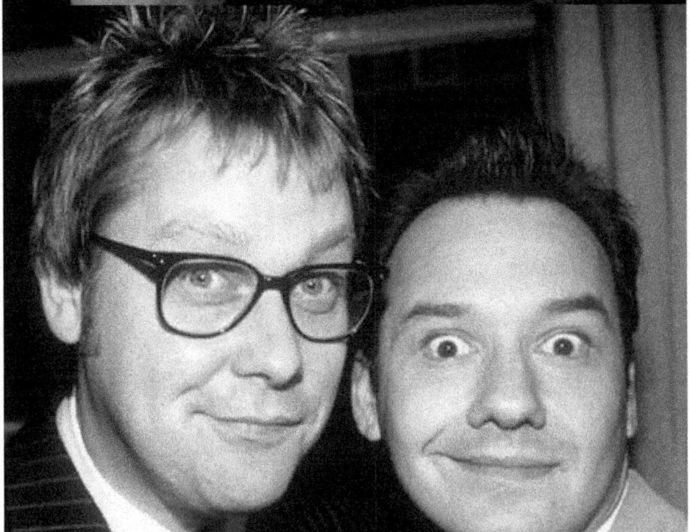

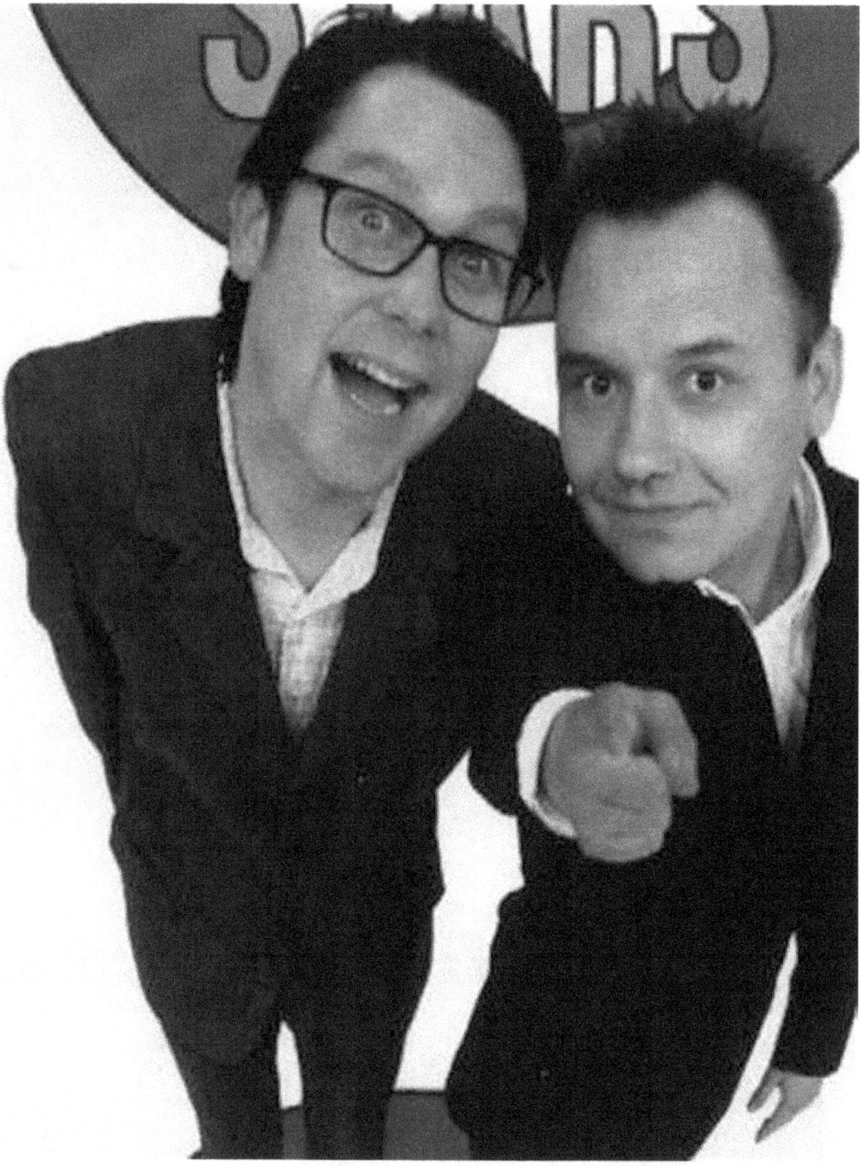

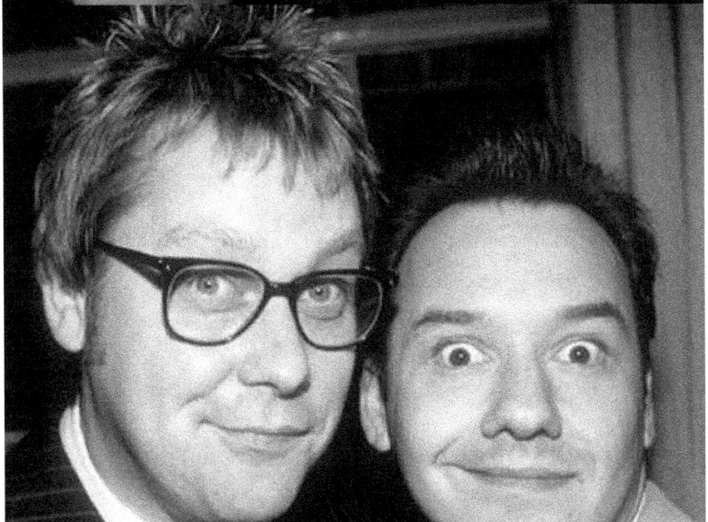

Lightning Source UK Ltd.
Milton Keynes UK
UKHW021033120522
402884UK00009B/663